First World War
and Army of Occupation
War Diary
France, Belgium and Germany

33 DIVISION
19 Infantry Brigade
Cameronians (Scottish Rifles)
5th Battalion
1 December 1915 - 30 September 1918

WO95/2422/3

The Naval & Military Press Ltd
www.nmarchive.com
Published in association with The National Archives

Published by

The Naval & Military Press Ltd

Unit 10 Ridgewood Industrial Park,

Uckfield, East Sussex,

TN22 5QE England

Tel: +44 (0) 1825 749494

www.naval-military-press.com

www.nmarchive.com

This diary has been reprinted in facsimile from the original. Any imperfections are inevitably reproduced and the quality may fall short of modern type and cartographic standards.

© Crown Copyright
Images reproduced by permission of The National Archives, London, England, 2015.

Contents

Document type	Place/Title	Date From	Date To
Heading	WO95/2422/3 5 Bn. Cameron 1945 (Royal Scottish Rides) 1915 Dec-1918 Sept.		
Heading	33 Division 19 Inf Bde 1/5 Scottish Rifles (Came Ronians) 1915 Dec-1918 Sep 1/6 Bn Ambl Comd With 5 Bn 1918 Oct From 2 Div 19 Bde.		
Heading	1/5 in Scottish Rifles Dec 1915 Vol XIV XXXIII Division		
Heading	War Diary Of 1/5th Scottish Rifle from 1st Decr To 31 Decr 1915.		
War Diary		01/12/1915	10/12/1915
War Diary		01/12/1915	26/12/1915
War Diary		12/12/1915	27/12/1915
Heading	1/5th Scottish Rifles. Jan XV. 33rd Div.		
War Diary		01/01/1916	08/01/1916
War Diary		01/01/1916	21/01/1916
War Diary		20/01/1916	31/01/1916
War Diary	Beuvry.	01/02/1916	29/02/1916
Heading	1/5 Scottish Rifles. Vol XVII.		
War Diary		01/03/1916	17/03/1916
War Diary		13/03/1916	31/03/1916
Heading	2/33 1/5 Scottish Rifles Vol XVIII.		
War Diary		01/04/1916	30/06/1916
Heading	19th Inf. Bde. 33rd Div. War Diary 5th Battn. The Cameronians (Scottish Rifles). July 1916.		
War Diary		01/07/1916	16/07/1916
War Diary		15/07/1916	31/07/1916
Heading	Appendices I, II & III.		
Miscellaneous	5th. Scottish Rifles War Diary, July 1916. Appendix I.	08/07/1916	08/07/1916
Map	Sketch Map Showing High Wood Etc.		
Miscellaneous	5th. Scottish Rifles War Diary, July 1916. Appendix III. 19th. Brigade.	23/07/1916	23/07/1916
Heading	19th Brigade 33rd Division. 1/5th Battalion Scottish Rifles August 1916.		
War Diary		01/08/1916	31/08/1916
Miscellaneous	Casualties for month were:-		
Operation(al) Order(s)	19th Infantry Brigade-Order No. 129. Appendix No. 1.	23/08/1916	23/08/1916
War Diary		01/09/1916	31/10/1916
Operation(al) Order(s)	19th. Infantry Brigade Order No. 167.	28/10/1916	28/10/1916
Miscellaneous	To "A" "D" Coy. Appendix II.		
War Diary		01/11/1916	31/03/1917
Miscellaneous	5th. Scottish Rifles.	30/03/1917	30/03/1917
War Diary		01/04/1917	31/05/1917
Miscellaneous	2/ Lt J.J. Scott. Wounded 21/5/17.	21/05/1917	21/05/1917
War Diary		01/06/1917	29/06/1917
Miscellaneous	5th Scottish Rifles.		
War Diary		01/07/1917	31/08/1917
Miscellaneous	Reinforcement Received During The Month.		
Miscellaneous	5th Scottish Rifles. September 1917. Vol 35.		
War Diary		01/10/1917	30/11/1917
Miscellaneous	5th Scottish Rifle Casualties During Month.		

War Diary		01/12/1917	31/03/1918
Heading	19th Brigade. 33rd Division. 1/5th Battalion Cameronians (Scottish Rifles) April 1918.		
War Diary		01/04/1918	16/04/1918
War Diary		15/04/1918	16/04/1918
War Diary		15/04/1918	17/04/1918
War Diary		16/04/1918	30/04/1918
Miscellaneous	C.B. 40.	12/04/1918	12/04/1918
Heading	War Diary. 5th Scottish Rifles. April, 1918. Appendix No. 2.		
Heading	War Diary. 5th Scottish Rifles. April, 1918. Appendix No. 1.		
Miscellaneous	B.M. 638.	13/04/1918	13/04/1918
Miscellaneous	My dear Spens.	20/04/1918	20/04/1918
Heading	War Diary. 5th Scottish Rifles. April, 1918. Appendix No. 3.		
Heading	Apps Listed 1-11 Missing (C).		
War Diary		01/05/1918	31/05/1918
War Diary		02/06/1918	30/06/1918
Miscellaneous	Casualties.		
War Diary	Brandhoek.	01/07/1918	31/07/1918
Miscellaneous	Casualties During Month.		
War Diary		01/08/1918	31/08/1918
Miscellaneous	Casualties during the month.		
War Diary	Le Souich.	01/09/1918	30/09/1918

WO 95 2422/3

5 Bn. Cameronians (Royal Scottish Rifles)
1915 Dec - 1918 Sept

33 DIVISION

19 INF BDE

1/5 SCOTTISH RIFLES (CAMERONIANS)

1915 DEC — 1918 SEP

1/6 BN AMALGAMATED WITH 5 BN
1918 OCT

FROM 2 DIV 1918 DE

19/33

1/5 in several Aufsätze

Dec 1915
vol XIV

XXXIII Dinner

Dec 15
Jan

1/13 H₂O
      g shah

Army Form C. 2118.

WAR DIARY
or
INTELLIGENCE SUMMARY.
(Erase heading not required.)

Confidential

War Diary
of
15th Scottish Rifles

from 1st Decr. to 31 Decr. 1915.

Army Form C. 2118.

WAR DIARY
or
INTELLIGENCE SUMMARY.

(Erase heading not required.)

Instructions regarding War Diaries and Intelligence Summaries are contained in F. S. Regs., Part II. and the Staff Manual respectively. Title pages will be prepared in manuscript.

Place	Date	Hour	Summary of Events and Information	Remarks and references to Appendices
	Dec 1st to Dec 10th 1915		In trenches at DUCKS BILL. The whole front covered with Mine Craters the near lip of the largest is held by us with Bombers. We have six days to hold. The weather is wretched and there is a great amount of flooding. The front trench had fallen in in places when we took over and continued to do so at irregular intervals from day to day. All hands are at work repairing and cleaning out trenches and communication trenches. The 18th Bn. Middlesex Regt., a Pioneer Battalion, are assisting the Brigade in keeping the water down, and the parapet up. Hostile sniping accounted for 2 men. On one day head – both killed. On 9th Decr. a mobile mine was exploded under one of the saplands and two men buried. One was rescued, but the other was dead before dug out. The mine did no material damage to the parapet and was thought to be a surface mine. We had one Company in front line, one in support and	

WAR DIARY
or
INTELLIGENCE SUMMARY.

(Erase heading not required.)

Army Form C. 2118.

Place	Date	Hour	Summary of Events and Information	Remarks and references to Appendices
	Dec. 1 to Dec. 10 1915.	(cont.)	two in Reserve. The front line Company was relieved daily. Much good work was done, and the trenches left in a much better condition than we had found them. The 6th R. Briggs relieved us on 10th Inst. Casualties during period:- 7739 L. Devlin, 9121 Lo Veitch, 6719 Pte Lauderdale, 7434 A. Sinclair, 6806 J. Drennan, all killed; twelve other ranks wounded.	
	Dec. 10		Marched to BETHUNE, and billeted in a new area for us near the Station. Found billets good. It is improbable to get Boots, we have only 16 pairs for the whole battalion, and no more are forthcoming in the meantime. We move to New Billets in Reserve Area "B" on 12th Inst.	
	Dec. 12		Moved to Billets at La Lenière, near LILLERS. Dropped four men sick on the road. Our packs were taken by Motor Wagon. Roads were flooded, and Battalion had to make a detour to reach	

WAR DIARY or INTELLIGENCE SUMMARY

Army Form C. 2118.

Place	Date	Hour	Summary of Events and Information	Remarks and references to Appendices
	1915 Dec 19		its destination. The Divisional G.O.C. saw us on road, and rode along the column making a detailed inspection. He had one or two faults to find in minor details such as boys hats &c, but made no comment on our march discipline. The Corps Commander on the march from trenches complimented one Company on its splendid appearance after 10 days in trenches.	
	Dec 20 to Dec 26		Weather cold & frosty, and flooding subsiding. There are about 4-5 hours training per day, and have submitted a programme of work for the week. To training of water in the Lewis Gun is proceeding. Lieut. Wilson has been appointed Brigade Grenade Officer and 2/Lt Clarkson succeeds him within. The Corps has ordered that there will be no leave for officers during the next period. We note from a recent home paper that 91608 Corpl. J.L. Dawson of the R.E. has won the V.C. at Hohenzollern Redoubt. He left this Battalion	

WAR DIARY
or
INTELLIGENCE SUMMARY.

(Erase heading not required.)

Army Form C. 2118.

Place	Date	Hour	Summary of Events and Information	Remarks and references to Appendices
	1915 Dec.13 to Dec.26		Battalion for the R.E. in July of this year. Billets are fair and are being improved. No hot baths are available, and no change of underclothing has yet been issued by the new Division. An epidemic of Diptheria has broken out. Two platoons are affected, and have been isolated. The Sanitary Authorities have taken the matter in hand, and everything is being done to prevent the spread of the disease. Up to 25. Jan't. we have 5 cases diagnosed and one suspected case. It is reported that the troops into previously occupied these Billets had suffered from sore throats, but no information as to this was handed over to us by the outgoing Battalion. Owing to wet weather and flooding, training has been hindered. Three route marches of about 3 or 4 hours duration have been done during the period. Work	

WAR DIARY
or
INTELLIGENCE SUMMARY.

Army Form C. 2118.

Place	Date	Hour	Summary of Events and Information	Remarks and references to Appendices
	(Dec 2)		Work has been done in improving the Billets in the way of making brick paths to latrines, and making Billets air tight. We handed over a drying room and a tile stove. There will be handed over to the incoming Battalion complete with all Sets of tools when we move. Lieut. P.S. Powell has been killed while attached to the Royal Flying Corps as an Observer. The machine fell from a height of 200 feet, and the cause of the fall has not been ascertained. This is the first casualty among our Commissioned ranks since coming to France, 13 months ago. Moved to BETHUNE, leaving the two isolated platoons behind. Good Billets for three days, and then moved on to ANNEQUIN FOSSE. LA BASSEE ROAD shelled daily. Some long shells landed in our Billets, killing a civilian woman, a horse, and a R.A.M.C. Private. One man of the Battalion was grazed by a piece of steel. Morning parades	

WAR DIARY
or
INTELLIGENCE SUMMARY.
(Erase heading not required.)

Army Form C. 2118.

Place	Date	Hour	Summary of Events and Information	Remarks and references to Appendices
			Parties have been sent to Trenches daily to clean up. On the night of 31st all was quiet, but our guns opened for a few minutes just at midnight.	

Summary

Effective strength 31/12/15 Officers 27 O.R.s 783
Reinforcements   "   75
Casualties :-   { 5 Killed, 12 Wounded }
                  45 sick
Cavalries :-

R. Suffrey Douglas Lieut. Col.
Commanding 1/5 Seaforth Hydrs (T)

15.O.
13 sheets

1/5th Scotish Rifles.

XV

33rd Div

WAR DIARY or INTELLIGENCE SUMMARY

Place	Date	Hour	Summary of Events and Information	Remarks and references to Appendices
	1916			
	1st Jany		Battalion is at ANNEQUIN FOSSE in Brigade Reserve. The Billets are subjected to a good deal of shelling. On 2nd January the Germans bombarded both sides of the LA BASSEE ROAD at CAMBRIN with considerable effect. A Shrapnel shell was put into a house containing a party coming from Rennes while the bombardment was going on and one man was killed. In billets one man was hurt by a piece of shell which struck a shell in his pocket but did not penetrate the case. Moved into trenches on 4th Jany and relieved the CAMERONIANS. We had the 2nd Royal Welsh Fusiliers on our left and a Cavalry Batt. of the 1st Dismounted Brigade on our right. Trenches are good but and very dilapidated. The wire on our front is poor and does not seem to have had much attention since the operations in September last. A large number of British dead are still lying between the lines in an advanced state of decomposition.	
	8th Jany			

WAR DIARY or INTELLIGENCE SUMMARY

Army Form C. 2118.

Place	Date	Hour	Summary of Events and Information	Remarks and references to Appendices
St Jan	1st Jany		B. St Jany. Our trenches were shelled for some time in the afternoon but no damage was done. In addition to our 2 Machine Guns we have 2 Lewis Guns with us and these are doing useful work in taking on snipers and hostile Machine Guns. We are in close touch with the Artillery and have a good working arrangement with them enabling us to get Artillery support at short notice. An officer checks a trouble sniper on St Jany and a stretcher was seen being brought up to take him away. The officer was using a periscope which had proved a most useful and safe weapon of offence in trenches. We have been notified that Territorial Battalions are to be brought up to establishment again and synony as General as we will now take one from Regular Battalions who are on equal strength and the loss of specialists will not be so much felt.	
St Jany				

WAR DIARY
INTELLIGENCE SUMMARY

Army Form C. 2118.

Place	Date	Hour	Summary of Events and Information	Remarks and references to Appendices
	1st Jany		One of our Captains has been sent to ETAPLES to assist in training of new formations for 2 months. I was working in the mess when accidentally shot from our own trenches, securing however a sight of my self have established complete fire superiority over the enemy and the co-operation of the Artillery with our trench guns and the movement of the Artillery were the Company hurries has kept the Huns very quiet indeed.	
	8th Jany		On the night of 1/8th Janury a man was wounded in the places while working on the wire.	
	9th Jany		The Battalion was relieved by the 1st Middlesex Regt. at 6:30 a.m. on 9th Jany and proceeded to billets at ANNEQUIN FOSSE moving thence to BETHUNE	
	10th Jany		In billets at ECOLE MICHELET BETHUNE. Billets are good and were found clean.	

WAR DIARY
or
INTELLIGENCE SUMMARY.
(Erase heading not required.)

Army Form C. 2118.

Place	Date	Hour	Summary of Events and Information	Remarks and references to Appendices
	10 Jany		The isolated platoon returned to the Battn today having been forced as there from infection. The Bum to BEUVRY to relieve the 2nd Royal Welch Fusiliers on 11th inst. Owing to one company of the 20th Royal Fusiliers being on duty at Corps Headquarters, one A Coy has been attached to that Battalion for French duty and is on Infantry at PONT FIXE. The C.O. left on 14th inst for London to be invested with the order of C.M.G. by His Majesty the King. This is the only decoration as medal which has come to the Officers of the Battn so far. The following Officers and men were mentioned in the Commander-in-Chiefs' last despatches.	
			Major A.A. KENNEDY	Sergt MACDONALD A.H.
			Capt. W.D. CROFT	" MACDONALD J.
			" J.M. GRIERSON	" MACLEAN J.
			Lieut GEO. GRAY	S.B. McGREGOR C.
	15 Jany			

WAR DIARY
OF
INTELLIGENCE=SUMMARY.
(Erase heading not required.)

Army Form C. 2118.

Place	Date	Hour	Summary of Events and Information	Remarks and references to Appendices
	16th Jany		The Battn. with the exception of "A" Coy. (they went out to PONT FIXE to support the 2nd Cyclist Fusiliers) were in BEUVRY NORTH as Brigade reserve and they were ready to turn out at an hour's notice by day & by night at half an hour's notice. The three Companies whilst here in BEUVRY carried on the usual training and experiments in marches under their Company Commanders. Machine Gunners and Stretcher also trained for the period under the Brigade Officer and M. Gun Officer. Lt. M.R. van Londo Gazette Lieut. A.H. Kemp's name appeared as 2nd Lieut., and he was duly posted to letter "D" Coy.	
	17th Jany		On this day the Battn moved up to the trenches taking over section of trenches just NORTH of the LA BASSEE CANAL	

WAR DIARY
or
INTELLIGENCE SUMMARY.
(Erase heading not required.)

Army Form C. 2118.

Place	Date	Hour	Summary of Events and Information	Remarks and references to Appendices
	19th Jany		and relieving the 2/6th Royal Fusiliers. On our right were the 1st CAMERONIANS and on our left the 1st KINGS. The trenches were very bad, a great number of the support and part of the fire trench were unused owing to the amount of water in them. The front line was very silent but had to be held in the centre of the section by detached posts following the battalion who held this section before, had done. The front we held amounted to about 150 yards, and this was absolutely untenable, the German trench were 3/400 yards away. During this period we had good weather and the enemy was quiet which enabled us to put out a good deal of wire on the trenches, and by the end of the week a great improvement had been made.	
	20th Jany			
	21st Jany			

WAR DIARY or INTELLIGENCE SUMMARY

Army Form C. 2118.

Place	Date	Hour	Summary of Events and Information	Remarks and references to Appendices
	20th Jany		We had pushed the communication trenches almost up & had strengthened the parapet and more. We had also cleared about 50 yards of the enemies part of the front line trench. On 20th Colonel Douglas went to 19th Bde H.Q. to take the place of General Robertson who was away on leave. Major A.A. KENNEDY took over command of the Battalion. On 20th we had two casualties in front line trench caused by a German rifle grenade coming into the trench, 5 of the men were wounded. On 23rd letter "C" and "D" Companies who were in the front line were relieved by letter "A" and "B" Companies from billets in PONT J'IX 13, the Companies relieved taking their place.	
	27th Jany			

WAR DIARY or INTELLIGENCE SUMMARY.

Army Form C. 2118.

Place	Date	Hour	Summary of Events and Information	Remarks and references to Appendices
	27th Jany		It was observed that the Enemy were more active probably owing to it being the KAISER'S birthday, and he shelled our trenches doing little or no damage however. We had no casualties. In the early morning the enemy attacked the Dismounted Cavalry but this attack was so weak that it was stopped.	
	28th Jany		The enemy opened a very violent bombardment on our trenches at about 10 A.M. which was continued until 4-30 P.M. with a break of an hour between and 2 o'clock. The enemy fire seemed to be concentrated on our 2nd line trenches and Communication trenches principally. Fortunately the second line trenches were reoccupied owing to the water in them but the Communication trenches were badly knocked in.	

WAR DIARY of INTELLIGENCE SUMMARY.

Army Form C. 2118.

Place	Date	Hour	Summary of Events and Information	Remarks and references to Appendices
	28th Jany.		We had only six casualties all of whom were only slightly hit. At night we were relieved by the 18th Royal Fusiliers and came back to BEUVRY NORTH as Brigade reserve to be ready to turn out by day on an hour and by night in half an hour. On arrival in billets we received a STAND TO message which lasted for 24 hours. In the event of attack we were to support "A" sector. 2nd Lieut South R.W.S. who arrived on night of 27th took up duty with Letter "B" Co. to-day.	
	29th Jany.		The Battalion supplied fatigue parties to clear trenches which were damaged by German bombardment.	
	30th Jany.		The men were all bathed and received clean underclothing. Rev. C. White (Capt.) took Church Parade in Cinema House BEUVRY.	

WAR DIARY
INTELLIGENCE SUMMARY.
(Erase heading not required.)

Army Form C. 2118.

Place	Date	Hour	Summary of Events and Information	Remarks and references to Appendices
	30th Jany.		In the afternoon we came under the call of the 98th Brigade in the event of an attack on Givenchy. We are under the orders of our own Brigade. 2/ Battalion had no word leaving and did short route marches under Company Commanders to harden their feet after being so long in trenches.	
	31st Jany.		The following awards appeared in London Gazette of 14th January.	
			Major KENNEDY A.A. a D.S.O.
			Lieut GRAY GEO. a Military Cross
			Sergt A.H. McDONALD a D.C.M.
			Sergt J. McDONALD a D.C.M.
			Pte. J. MacLEAN a D.C.M.
			L.B. C. McGREGOR a D.C.M.

WAR DIARY
or
INTELLIGENCE SUMMARY.

Army Form C. 2118.

Place	Date	Hour	Summary of Events and Information	Remarks and references to Appendices
	31st Jany		On 25th 2nd Lieut GEO. GRAY left us to be attached to 1st Wing as Flying Instructor. On 30th 2nd Lieut. E.G. DAVIES left to attend Divisional School at VERDUN for 10 days course. **SUMMARY** Effective strength as at 31st January 1916: 30 Officers and 481 other ranks. Reinforcement during January: 36 other ranks and 1 Officer, also one Officer promoted from the ranks. **CASUALTIES** Sick 41 other ranks. Wounded 12 other ranks. Killed 2 other ranks. R. Jeffray Douglas Lt Col Comdg 9/620 Rifles.	

WAR DIARY
or
INTELLIGENCE SUMMARY.
(Erase heading not required.)

Army Form C. 2118.

Place	Date	Hour	Summary of Events and Information	Remarks and references to Appendices
BEUVRY	FEB.1st		Training was carried out by companies, and short route marches were done. Orders were received that the Battalion would proceed tomorrow to BOURECQ marching to BETHUNE thence by rail to LILLERS and continuing by road to BOURECQ. Here we were to stay one night then proceed to billets WEST OF BOSNES for divisional training. This order was cancelled late in the evening and orders were received to stand fast.	
Do.	FEB. 2nd		The M.O. inspected the last two drafts 22nd and 24th January and states that their physique was fair, but that many suffered from rheumatism and similar complaints. Also that one man was minus a thumb on his right hand.	
Do.	FEB.3rd&4th		Company and specialist training was carried out as usual.	
Do.	FEB.5th		Training as usual. A Battalion concert managed by the Chaplain and held in the Cinema House was most successful.	
Do.	FEB.6th		Church Parade was held in the Cinema House also a short service at 6 p.m. Short route marches were performed by Companies after Church Parade.	

WAR DIARY
or
INTELLIGENCE SUMMARY.
(Erase heading not required.)

Army Form C. 2118.

Place	Date	Hour	Summary of Events and Information	Remarks and references to Appendices
	FEB 7th		The Battalion moved to trenches in Z.O. sector relieving the 2nd WORCEST. Regiment. This sector contained a crater which was taken from the Germans a few nights ago by the 2nd R.W.F. Our bombers hold the crater. A Company of 20th R.F. supported us in WIMPOLE STREET. The 1st Americans were on our right and on the left the 19th R.F. The trenches in this sector were not in good condition being very wet and muddy.	
	FEB 8th		On account of our small numbers both of men and officers available it was decided by the C.O. to stop leave till 13th inst. "B" Coy on the right were much troubled by Minnenwerfers and trench mortars and we replied with artillery. The usual work was done on trenches.	
	FEB 9th		The Brigadier inspected the trenches. "B" Coy were again troubled by Minnenwerfers etc. The usual work was continued.	

WAR DIARY
or
INTELLIGENCE SUMMARY.

(Erase heading not required.)

Army Form C. 2118.

Place	Date	Hour	Summary of Events and Information	Remarks and references to Appendices
	Feb 10th/12th		Hostile Mortars were responsible for a number of Casualties but were kept under by our Artillery. The Mortar position was located. A draft of 51 men arrived on 10th inst. They were of a good type. Owing to our having the craters to hold our expenditure of grenades is heavy and parties are carrying grenades daily. A Company of 4th Lincolns was attached for 48 hours for training.	
	Feb 12th		Battalion was relieved by 20th R.F. 2 platoons being left in the Keeps on relief the Battalion was Billeted in ANNEQUIN FOSSE.	
	Feb 13th to 16th Feb		While at the FOSSE working parties were out all day doing mining fatigues and cleaning communication trenches. No opportunities for training were afforded. Batts were arranged but only a few men were able to avail themselves of these owing to so many working parties being required.	

Army Form C. 2118.

WAR DIARY
or
INTELLIGENCE SUMMARY.
(Erase heading not required.)

Instructions regarding War Diaries and Intelligence Summaries are contained in F.S. Regs., Part II. and the Staff Manual respectively. Title pages will be prepared in manuscript.

Place	Date	Hour	Summary of Events and Information	Remarks and references to Appendices
	Feb 16th		Battalion relieved 20th Royal Fusiliers in the same section on the evening of the 16th inst.	
	Feb 17th to 19th Feb.		Conditions were pretty much the same. Mortars and rifle grenades caused some casualties. Two men were killed by one of our own shells. Weather was bad and gum boots were worn all the time. Considerable improvement was made on the R.W.F. crater and saps were cut out to it and listening posts cut into the lip of the crater. The Brigadier visited the trenches twice during this tour. On the 19th about 10 a.m. one of our aeroplanes was brought down in our trenches. The pilot escaped but the machine was smashed by hostile shelling which opened almost as soon as the machine had landed. Battalion was relieved on night of 19th by the 20th Royal Fusiliers	

1577 Wt.W10791/1773 50,000 1/15 D. D. & L. A.D.S.S./Forms/C. 2118

WAR DIARY
or
INTELLIGENCE SUMMARY.

(Erase heading not required.)

Army Form C. 2118.

Place	Date	Hour	Summary of Events and Information	Remarks and references to Appendices
	Feb 19th		who had a Company of Munsters attached for instruction. The relief took about 5 hours. Battalion went to ANNEQUIN FOSSE in relief.	
	Feb 20th to 22nd Feb.		Moved to LE QUESNOY at 10 am on 20th. Found billets good but very dirty. At LE QUESNOY we remained in support of our own Brigade. The wind has gone round to the East and special precautions against gas have been ordered. On 21st there was a very heavy bombardment all day in the vicinity of LOOS.	
	22nd Feb		Moved to HINGETTE where we were billeted in farms. Heavy snow storm on the way. Ground is covered with snow and training is consequently hampered. Lewis Gun and Grenade Classes have been started with the idea of training every man in these branches.	

Army Form C. 2118.

WAR DIARY
or
INTELLIGENCE SUMMARY.
(Erase heading not required.)

Instructions regarding War Diaries and Intelligence Summaries are contained in F. S. Regs., Part II. and the Staff Manual respectively. Title pages will be prepared in manuscript.

Place	Date	Hour	Summary of Events and Information	Remarks and references to Appendices
	FEB 22nd		Our Machine Gun section has been disbanded and the men have been sent to their companies as riflemen. The Machine Gun Officer has also been attached to a company.	
	FEB. 28th		Moved to LE QUESNOY where we found the billets in an indescribable state of filth. All the billet stores were lost and the Warden had nothing to issue.	
	FEB 29th		Had baths at BEUVRY and clean clothing. We go to trenches A.I. on 1st March being relieved by 6th Scottish Rifles.	
			Summary	
			Effective strength as at 29th February 1916 %42 Other ranks	
			Reinforcements during February 2 Officers 24 Officers	
			51 Other ranks	
			Casualties, killed 9	
			Wounded 16	
			Sick 54	

1577 Wt. W10791/1773 50,000 1/15 D. D. & L. A.D.S.S./Forms/C. 2118.

X̶X̶X̶I̶I̶I̶ 2/83

(19/47)

1/5 Scottish Rifles
Vol XVII

WAR DIARY
or
INTELLIGENCE SUMMARY.

(Erase heading not required.)

Army Form C. 2118.

Place	Date	Hour	Summary of Events and Information	Remarks and references to Appendices
	1st Mar. 1916		Battalion relieved 1st Queen's Regt. in trenches at A1 CUINCHY SECTION. The Camerons are on our left and the 4th Kings, a battalion of the 98th Brigade on our right. We have 2 Companies in the first line, one in support and one in reserve. Battalion Hdqrs. are in HARLEY STREET. Owing to time being taken up in fitting on gum boots the relief was a slow one. Trenches were found in good condition and well preserved. We have one crater ap, which goes right through a small British crater to the lip of a large German one. It is not held during the day as the large crater can be observed from the flanks.	
	3rd Mar. 1916		During the night snow fell heavily and the ground is now white. It continues to snow. The trenches have been kept fresh swept by the snow storm. In many parts they are falling in and there is much mud and water in the communication trenches.	

WAR DIARY
or
INTELLIGENCE SUMMARY.
(Erase heading not required.)

Army Form C. 2118.

Place	Date	Hour	Summary of Events and Information	Remarks and references to Appendices
	3rd Mar. 1916		Our own Trench mortars succeeded in landing 3 bombs in our trenches, two of which were "duds", and the third in exploding wounded one of our men. The further activities of this particular Battery for the night were stopped by Regiment. We have 2 observation posts where special observers are stationed all day. They have been able to indicate numerous targets to the Artillery and have tapped some German signal messages which however have not been deciphered. The observers keep a log book in which they record the days observations and these are included in the daily intelligence report to the Brigade.	
	4th Mar. 1916		We have been supplied with a number of green rockets, for use when a gas attack is launched by the enemy. They will furnish a speedy warning for all parties in rear and for the Artillery. Owing to the snow white suits were issued to men who went out on patrol.	

WAR DIARY or INTELLIGENCE SUMMARY

Army Form C. 2118.

Place	Date	Hour	Summary of Events and Information	Remarks and references to Appendices
	5th Mar. 1916		All hands engaged in cleaning trenches, building-up fallen-in portions and revetting. Weather conditions are severe and telling severely on the front line Companies there being insufficient dug-outs to provide cover for the men. Special orders have been issued with regard to the arresting of anybody known as a number of spies have recently been allowed to escape through carelessness. The support and reserve Companies relieved the front line Companies this morning. A test gas alarm was carried through by order of the Brigade. All men were ready and in their proper positions in 3 minutes from the time of receiving the message. The Artillery co-operated promptly except in the case of one Battery which could not be informed owing to the condition of the wires or inattention on the part of their telephonists. The tube helmets used on this test were returned and exchanged for new ones on the following day.	

WAR DIARY or INTELLIGENCE SUMMARY.

Army Form C. 2118.

Place	Date	Hour	Summary of Events and Information	Remarks and references to Appendices
	7th Mar 1916		A small defensive mine was exploded by our miners in front of Boyau 32. All our front line troops were drawn back to a distance of 200 yards when the mine was blown and they immediately occupied the front line trenches thereafter. The enemy shelled our trenches slightly but their infantry made no action. A sap is being dug out to the craters which is about 30 yards in front of our existing sap. The crater has been patrolled nightly and no sign of the enemy trying to sap to it have been found. Owing to heavy sniping it has been impossible to proceed quickly with the sap which is being dug from the inside. The line held by the Brigade has been shortened allowing 1 Battalion to go out of trenches. This has necessitated our putting a 3rd Company in the front line and taking over some trenches on our right while vacating some on our left.	
	8th Mar. 1916			

WAR DIARY
or
INTELLIGENCE SUMMARY.
(Erase heading not required.)

Army Form C. 2118.

Place	Date	Hour	Summary of Events and Information	Remarks and references to Appendices
	8th Mar. 1916		The section is now from Bogan 32 and is known as A1. The change necessitated a complicated relief which started at 5 p.m. and finished at midnight. It leaves the Brigade with 2 Battalions in and 2 not in support. One Company of the 20th R.F. has taken over the duty of Battalion reserve. We now have 3 Companies in front line, 1 in support and 1 in Reserve. The Royal Welsh Fusiliers are on our left and the 16th K.R.R's on our right. Small defensive mine blows on our extreme right. Companies were withdrawn as before. Sap as being dug by K.R.R's. Our patrol went round the new crater and met a German patrol of greater strength than their own. Our patrol was armed with bombs and revolvers but patrols were too far apart to allow of these being used. A known officer from the Artillery sleeps at Bn. HdQrs every night.	
	9th Mar. 1916			

WAR DIARY or INTELLIGENCE SUMMARY

Army Form C. 2118.

Place	Date	Hour	Summary of Events and Information	Remarks and references to Appendices
	10th Mar. 1916		Our patrols continue to do useful work and have been out every night. The craters on our front have been carefully explored and much information gained. Weather has hampered work in the trenches and all hands are engaged in clearing and cleaning.	
	11th Mar. 1916		C.O. and officers of 20th Royal Fusiliers visited trenches to-day in view of relief to-morrow.	
	12th Mar. 1916		Rifle grenade killed one man and wounded 4 others. Our No 3 rifle grenades were defective and many of them failed to burst. Battalion was relieved by 20th Royal Fusiliers, relief commencing at 6-30 p.m. Owing to having to change our gun traps, the relief was not completed till about 2 a.m. One Company remained in reserve and the remaining 3 moved to Le Quesnoy.	
	13th Mar. 1916 to 17th Mar. 1916		All ranks were bathed and had an issue of clean clothing. Daily parties are being supplied for work on the reserve trenches near LE QUESNOY under the R.E.	

WAR DIARY or INTELLIGENCE SUMMARY

Army Form C. 2118.

Place	Date	Hour	Summary of Events and Information	Remarks and references to Appendices
Bethune	13th Mar 1916		All the defences behind the lines are being strengthened and a great quantity of barbed wire is being put up. The C.O. completed a draft of 34 N.C.O. & Men which arrived on 14th Feby. 1916. We have received a number of officers as reinforcements and we are now 1 over strength in Commissioned ranks. Every a Captain having arrived from the 3/5th who was senior to one of our Captains, the Command of Coy. had to be altered. Battalion moved to Bethune on 17th March.	
			I was billeted in Rue D'Aire. The Company attached to 20th Royal Fusiliers joined the Battalion late in the evening. Billets were good and had been left clean. This is the first time the Battalion has been billeted in town since January. On the night of 19/20th the Battn was ordered to stand to and all men were confined to Barracks. Heavy firing was heard and gas was reported by the Hdqrs. Guard sentry. The Germans were attacking near the Hohenzollern Redoubt	
	17th Mar 1916			

WAR DIARY or INTELLIGENCE SUMMARY

Army Form C. 2118.

Place	Date	Hour	Summary of Events and Information	Remarks and references to Appendices
	17th Mar. 1916		The following morning orders were received that men need no longer be confined to Billets but that they must remain within easy call. Special orders have been issued in connection with the wearing of kilts and general cleanliness while in town. It was anticipated that the Division was coming out of the line and was to move back to a rest area for this reason Companies did route marching in full marching order to get men's feet hardened.	
	19th Mar. 1916		Church Parade was held in the replenished Chapel fue d'Aire and was conducted by Rev. Major Stewart in the absence of our own Padre on leave. The Rev. Stewart is the Padre who first conducted a service for the Battⁿ on its arrival in France. All fur coats and leather jerkins were returned to store but were subsequently withdrawn when it became known that we were to go back to trenches. Battalion relieved 1/6th Scottish Rifles in Anchy Right subsection	
	24th Mar. 1916			

WAR DIARY or INTELLIGENCE SUMMARY

Army Form C. 2118.

Place	Date	Hour	Summary of Events and Information	Remarks and references to Appendices
	24th Mar. 1916	at 6-30 p.m.	Owing to the long march from BETHUNE tea was taken at BEUVRY from which Platoons moved at 100 yards interval to trenches. The line was held with 10 Platoons in the front line, 3 Platoons in support and 3 Platoons in reserve 1 of which was a Railway Keep. The 1st Queens were on our left and the 12th Lancers on our right. There is a new German crater on this front which is right on the German parapet. Our patrols reported on it and on the wire round it. During this shell in trenches our observers who had 3 hoops got much useful information and were able to anticipate a rifle of the troops opposite no which the artillery dealt with. A large shrapnel was brought up by the enemy and knocked in two of our sapps and about 20 feet of front line parapet. Difficulty was found in getting retaliation from the distillery who had orders to economise. This big Hennie was evidently taken away as it only fired on two days.	

Place	Date	Hour	Summary of Events and Information	Remarks and references to Appendices
	27th Mar. 1916		Our snipers accounted for 2 Germans during the day in trenches. The left company B Coy. was much bombed with rifle grenades which however very nearly and caused some casualties.	
	28th Mar. 1916		We were relieved by the 20th Royal Fusiliers on 28th and billeted for the night at ANNEQUIN SOUTH. The following day (29th) we moved to BETHUNE after relief by the 16th Yorks & Lancs. Regt. much Battalion attached to our Brigade for instruction. Billets in BETHUNE were ECOLE DE JEUNES FILLES and ECOLE MICHELET both of which are good billets. It was impossible to get baths as they were booked up by the 100th Brigade.	
	31st Mar. 1916		The weather has now become brilliant and spring seems to have started in earnest. The C.O. inspected 100 men who arrived from 3/5th on 29th inst. They were older than our average man and their equipment was filthy. They will require to have discipline rubbed into them.	

Army Form C. 2118.

WAR DIARY
or
INTELLIGENCE SUMMARY.
(Erase heading not required.)

Place	Date	Hour	Summary of Events and Information	Remarks and references to Appendices
	31st Mar. 1916		Companies did route marching and Bayonet fighting and men received further training in the Lewis Gun.	
			Total strength at 31st March 35 Officers. 873 other ranks	
			Arrived during month 5 " 134 men	
			Casualties " " 51 Sick (other ranks)	
			24 Wounded (") of which 1 died in Hospital	
			4 Killed (other ranks)	

R. Aubrey Douglas Lieut-Col.
Commanding 1/5th Seaforth Rifles

3rd April 1916.

2/33

1/5 Scottish Rifles

Vol XVIII

Army Form C. 2118.

WAR DIARY
or
INTELLIGENCE SUMMARY.
(Erase heading not required.)

Place	Date	Hour	Summary of Events and Information	Remarks and references to Appendices
	April 1st		Moved to Annequin South and took over billets of 16th Notts & Derby Regiment	
	to 4th		Working parties to R.E. for mining and carrying during the whole period.	
	4th		Battalion relieved 16th Notts & Derby Regiment in Cuinchy right Subsection. The Companies were in our left and 12th Division on our right. Battalion went to 650 strong and 16th were an additional portion of the support line next to our station. At midnight 6 mines were blown by our miners on our right. Rebuilding of parapets commenced and general repairs work throughout the Subsection. Enemy fired rifle grenade batteries have been most successful and have wounded in keeping the enemy quiet. We took over a new portion of line from 12 Division with the platoon about 1/2 man amount went into just South of the Hohenzollern Redoubt followed by Coy. Meeting but our section was not shelled. Lots partly of Germans were seen by our snipers and the Germans were hard at there use of our men were slightly wounded one by shrapnel and one by a rifle grenade. Cert Snipers claim a victim today.	
	6th		At 7am enemy shelled our support line running trying to knock out our	

15.O.
9 sheets

WAR DIARY or INTELLIGENCE SUMMARY.

Army Form C. 2118.

(Erase heading not required.)

Instructions regarding War Diaries and Intelligence Summaries are contained in F. S. Regs., Part II. and the Staff Manual respectively. Title pages will be prepared in manuscript.

Place	Date	Hour	Summary of Events and Information	Remarks and references to Appendices
	April 6th		Rifle grenade batteries. Line was considerable total strength throughout the day, which however caused us no material damage. We had one man killed and 3 wounded by rifle grenades. Our snipers again claim 2 victims.	
	7th		Battalion were relieved by 2 Coys 21st Royal Scots and two Coys 11th H.L.I. Relief being completed by 10.20 p.m. Just before relief a rifle grenade fell into one of our dugouts wounding 2 of our men. Battn Hd Qrs Lt Col George Hy Gunn Jameson: Bethune: Rallying Post: Coy at Barry.	
	8th		In Bethune. Billets good. Remained for 2 days and moved to OBLINGHEM on 10th April.	
	10th		Battalion marched as a Battalion and was quite strong in numbers. At a moment we are the strongest Battalion in the Brigade. Billets at Oblinghen are scattered but generally good. Beds have been erected in a number of billets and more have been put in by us. All the ground in the vicinity of billets is under cultivation and a training ground for the Battalion was found about 1½ miles away. While at Oblinghen the G.O.C. 33rd Division inspected the billets. He took special notice of the cookers and enquired	

T.134. Wt. W708-776. 500000. 4/15. Sir J.C. & S.

Army Form C. 2118.

WAR DIARY
or
INTELLIGENCE SUMMARY.
(Erase heading not required.)

Instructions regarding War Diaries and Intelligence Summaries are contained in F. S. Regs., Part II. and the Staff Manual respectively. Title pages will be prepared in manuscript.

Place	Date	Hour	Summary of Events and Information	Remarks and references to Appendices
	April 10th		About the kind and variety of food given to the men. He ordered that field ovens should be built, so that meals might be prepared. The G.O.C. 19th Brigade also inspected the Battalion. 7 Transport during this period. With Capt Offingham a test alarm was carried through. Battalion was ready to move in 1 hour & 40 minutes. Draft of 50 arrived.	
	15th		Moved to Billets for the night. C.O. and Coy Commanders visited the Trenches at Curinchy Right Subsector.	
	17th		Took over from 1/6th Scottish Rifles in Curinchy Right Subsector. On the way from Bethune we were taken at Beuvry. In spite of wet weather few feet were sore necessary and relief was completed under 2 hours.	
	18th		About 8 am Trenches were heavily bombarded by Minenwerfer. About 35 trench Mortars came into our section. The Telephonist's dug out was bombed and 2 others wounded. Captain Russel and two Stretcher bearers were killed and the men traced. Effective Artillery retaliation could not be pressed. During the rest of the day the enemy was quiet. Between 11 and 12 midnight we exploded a mine to the left of our Sector.	
	19th			

T.J.134. W.t. W708—776. 500000. 4/15. Sir J. C. & S.

WAR DIARY
or
INTELLIGENCE SUMMARY.
(Erase heading not required.)

Army Form C. 2118.

Instructions regarding War Diaries and Intelligence Summaries are contained in F. S. Regs., Part II. and the Staff Manual respectively. Title pages will be prepared in manuscript.

Place	Date	Hour	Summary of Events and Information	Remarks and references to Appendices
	20th April		At 4.45 am the enemy exploded a mine just North of our Sector. No damage was done and no notice by the enemy developed. Sapping platoon have been working in our Sector making a new tunnel and clearing and old one. Sergeant — was shaved about 2 pm and 3 other Ots were detained. The Birle shoots were off for 48 hrs dinner. A red, white and red flag has been spotted by our observers on a tree on the La Bassée Road being the enemy. It is thought to be the boundary mark of a Hunt and is being kept under observation. Sand bag covers have been made for Not details so it was found that they were the confusion. At 9.30 pm the German Trenches on our left were heavily bombarded by artillery and trench mortar batteries. After the bombardment a party of the Canadians entered the enemy's lots but they were found empty and the party returned without topics of information.	
	21st "		At 4 am the enemy exploded a small mine immediately on our right that however did no damage. It transpired that they had blown up some of their own men in the process as they were seen trying to recover a man by	

WAR DIARY
or
INTELLIGENCE SUMMARY.
(Erase heading not required.)

Army Form C. 2118.

Instructions regarding War Diaries and Intelligence Summaries are contained in F. S. Regs., Part II. and the Staff Manual respectively. Title pages will be prepared in manuscript.

Place	Date	Hour	Summary of Events and Information	Remarks and references to Appendices
	21st April		The Coys. A. Rents. left grounds hard previously and won not done. Our Snipers have been disappointed as there is no sign of the enemy (looking over the trenches and they cannot get any targets. At 10.35/m we had a test gas alarm. Average time before all Coys were ready 3 minuts. Artillery fired in 55 rounds. Schrafs were kept on by all ranks for 50 minuts without discomfort.	
	22nd		Trenches very wet. All Coys busy baling. Working Support trenches shelled by Field guns & Howitzs and knocked in several places. A draft of 30 men arrived from 3/5th Lee. Rifle. Battalion was relieved by 2nd D.W. Fusiliers and went to billets at Annequin North. The Coy. remained in support to the 2nd D.W.F.	
	23rd		Billets fair. Partially the whole Battalion out on working parties for R.E. Owing to the change of staff Colonels becoming early weather it has been necessary to have the holding road quite finished this has been done. A patrol report has been sent back to us with the Divisional Commanders comments on it thus "A very well conducted patrol"	

WAR DIARY
or
INTELLIGENCE SUMMARY.
(Erase heading not required.)

Army Form C. 2118.

Place	Date	Hour	Summary of Events and Information	Remarks and references to Appendices
	23rd April		I hope it will lead to good results. Patrol was lead by 2/Lt Lang.	
	24th		Work carried on in bivouac unimproved. New post in and shell shelter built. During the day the enemy sent over some heavy shells in the Battalion Sector of the La Bassée Road. Weather brilliant and surprising.	
	25th		The 2nd R.W.F. at 6.5 a heavy bombardment made a raid on German trench which was fairly successful, made a good number of prisoners. Owing to the wire not having been properly cut at one point the R.W.F.s had a number of casualties.	
	26th		Relieved 2nd R.W.F. in Curraghy Right Subsection with Cameronian on our left and 100th Brigade on our right. A great deal of machine gun fire at night. We left open the gap in enemy's wire. There was a very heavy bombardment going on in the direction of Loos	
	27/4		At 5am very heavy bombardment in South. There received that enemy were using gas at Hulluck. Gas was seen on our front but it did not affect our section. The artillery got most of it and kno out succeeded. It was learned that the Germans had	

WAR DIARY
or
INTELLIGENCE SUMMARY

Army Form C. 2118.

Place	Date	Hour	Summary of Events and Information	Remarks and references to Appendices
	27th April		Captured 300 yards of trench but that they had been ejected in half an hour. At 12.30 p.m. the enemy with 5 Bombers went out and bombed the enemy posts at Suffolk Crater. The crater was strongly held and a good bomb fight resulted as rifle grenades were covering the party. The enemy fired his machine guns and put up 2 red stars. Then we suffered no casualties.	
	28 "		Heat still continues. Enemy's Artillery has been active registering on reserve trenches. A forward Gun team was seen in the evening which turned out to be without gunsubation. Heavy firing was heard in the south.	
	29 d "		Early this was heavy shelled during the evening and several direct hits obtained on the Field Ambulance Station. At 11pm a pre-arranged Bombardment of the enemy front line and Craters commenced. Troops were withdrawn from our front line and a good deal of damage done to the hostile trenches. Lieut McEwan was slightly wounded in the hand by a fragment of shell	

Army Form C. 2118.

WAR DIARY
or
INTELLIGENCE SUMMARY.
(Erase heading not required.)

Instructions regarding War Diaries and Intelligence Summaries are contained in F. S. Regs., Part II. and the Staff Manual respectively. Title pages will be prepared in manuscript.

Place	Date	Hour	Summary of Events and Information	Remarks and references to Appendices
	30th April		The enemy replied to our bombardment of last night by shelling with heavy Maunsergen field guns & howitzers. Officers casualties were relieved by 2nd R.W.F. at 8pm. Relief was completed in 1 hour. Battalion after relief was billeted at Annequin North.	
			Summary	
			Total strength at date — 34 Officers 885 Other Ranks	
			Carried during month — 96 D:	
			Casualties —	
			1 Officer killed	
			1 D: Wounded	
			1 D: D: (Remained at duty)	
			50 Other Ranks wounded (13 Remained at duty)	
			14 Other Ranks killed in action	

A.R. Kennedy / Major
Comm 5th S.W.B.

T2134. Wt. W708-776. 500000. 4/15. Sir J.C. & S.

WAR DIARY or INTELLIGENCE SUMMARY

1/5 Scottish Rifles

Place	Date	Hour	Summary of Events and Information	Remarks and references to Appendices
	1916			
	1st May		While at Annequin North the whole Battalion was employed on working parties for the R.E. Improvements were made to billets & the Artillery of walls commenced. On the evening of 3rd May it was reported that signalling by lamp had been seen in Annequin. The A.P.M. arrived about midnight & a search was made in two suspected houses but no information was got. Just before 1 o'clock a.m. the enemy shelled the village with 5" shells, one of which accounted for five other ranks (3 dangs & 2 men) one Sergt was killed. Battalion was relieved by 1st Middlesex Regt & moved to Oblinghem.	E.N. 19.O. 5 Mar
	4th		Billets at Oblinghem good. Overhead wires in most of the village to prevent aeroplane landing. Billets are being fitted with distemper inside & improves the lighting & appearance of Billets & makes them cleaner & healthier. Training in new carried on as per programs submitted to the Division. Coys in turn take day about found up as strong as possible so as to get the Section Commanders experience in working their commands at full strength	
	5th			

WAR DIARY or INTELLIGENCE SUMMARY.

(Erase heading not required.)

Instructions regarding War Diaries and Intelligence Summaries are contained in F. S. Regs., Part II. and the Staff Manual respectively. Title pages will be prepared in manuscript.

Place	Date	Hour	Summary of Events and Information	Remarks and references to Appendices
	10th May		On 10th May there was a Brigade Route march of about 8 miles. The Major General Commanding the Division inspected the Brigade as it marched past and we had no fault to find. The Transport-Vehicles had all been freshly painted and looked very well. The men too are on the whole. In the evening a Brigade Boxing Tournament was held in Bethune. We had several entries and men did well against the regular soldiers. The men were in the final of the Heavy-weight & got 2nd Prize. 2nd Lt Treepe from 3/5th Leicesters Rgt. joined on 12th May and was posted to A Coy. The period of its Brigade in trenches has been increased to 24 days on 12 days out. For this reason the Battalion remained at Allouagne till	
	16th "		16th May & then moved to Beuvry for the first 6 days of the Brigade spell. We will relieve the 3rd Royal Welsh Fusiliers on every night. Subsection etc. as we go in. At Beuvry Billets good. Working parties are being sent to the trenches daily & the Pioneers are busy making Afro-roads	

WAR DIARY
or
INTELLIGENCE SUMMARY.

Army Form C. 2118.

Place	Date	Hour	Summary of Events and Information	Remarks and references to Appendices
			I generally improved and referring the Biscuits turning to the heat bothering too again started 7 each day parties go down to the Canal where a bathing place has been arranged for them. One man was killed on a wire party on the 19 instant. On the night of 21st a cloud of tear gas passed over Beauty I had the effect of causing the eyes to water. The Gas was quite thick and came from the South where the enemy had been using gas shells.	
	22nd May		On 22nd Battn relieved 2nd Royal Welsh Fusiliers in Andy right and left & the 7th Camerons & 5th Seaforth on our right. The Camerons were on our left & the 7th Camerons & 5th Seaforth on our right. The section was found to be much quieter than on former occasion. It was reported that Mayor Jago's were opposite us. Our Rifle Grenade Battery reinforced by those of the 2nd Royal Welsh Fusiliers kept the enemy's rifle grenades from firing as we always sent back about 12 for 1. We had a battery of 16 ready to fire on offered targets at any time. The Lewis Guns	

WAR DIARY
INTELLIGENCE SUMMARY.
(Erase heading not required.)

Army Form C. 2118.

Instructions regarding War Diaries and Intelligence Summaries are contained in F. S. Regs., Part II. and the Staff Manual respectively. Title pages will be prepared in manuscript.

Place	Date	Hour	Summary of Events and Information	Remarks and references to Appendices
	27		were engaged in digging them after we the battle. were not taking prisoners considering German. We had one French mortar in the shelter - a British 60 pounder to the right of H/1 we captured 2 men we found of the Germans one of which was thought to have been a member of Cavalier to the enemy army to the meaning of here which meant the distance at night the ammunition used were between by 300 yds. During the period our Divisions were visited by a Russian officer Lieut George Grey, reported the return of the military bars from General Munro at a french later action of on Bethune officers.	
	28		Royal Scots Fusiliers on 28th inst moved to Billets in Annequin South. took to at Annequin Bath. who ready to move at 5 hours notice, with one Company on 5 minutes notice working parties were supplied daily for the R.E. A draft of 100 men joined us at Annequin South. They had arrived after dep. Battery and were left at Bouvry to be trained in the	

T.2134. Wt. W708—776. 500000. 4/16. Sir J. C. & S.

WAR DIARY or INTELLIGENCE SUMMARY

Army Form C. 2118.

Place	Date	Hour	Summary of Events and Information	Remarks and references to Appendices

1st Batt. Scots Guards. There was a further draft of 66 men from 1/6th Scottish Rifles which Battalion has been split up amongst to the difficulty of getting out drafts from Home. Battalion is now at full strength but some officers are still required to bring us up to 43. Nine officers arrived from 3/5th Scottish Rifles on 31st inst. and were posted to the companies for duty. They are all junior officers. Some of them having been out with the Batt. in France as N.C.Os.

Summary

Total strength at date — 1019
Arrived during March — 141 O.R. and 10 Officers
Casualties — 9 Killed, 44 Wounded, 53 Sick.

R. Gipps Douglas
Lt.Col.
Comdg. 1st Scots Gds Rifles

1/5 Scott. Rifles
Vol 20

20.0
6 sheets

WAR DIARY

~~INTELLIGENCE SUMMARY.~~

(Erase heading not required.)

Army Form C. 2118.

Instructions regarding War Diaries and Intelligence Summaries are contained in F. S. Regs., Part II. and the Staff Manual respectively. Title pages will be prepared in manuscript.

Place	Date	Hour	Summary of Events and Information	Remarks and references to Appendices
	1st.June,1916.		ANNEQUIN SOUTH. The Fosse was heavily shelled during the greater part of the day without material damage being done. We continue to supply working parties for the R.E. daily. Owing to lack of material work on billet improvement has been hampered, but rifle racks have been made for some billets and shell shelters improved.	
	3rd.June,1916.		Relieved 2nd. Royal Welsh Fusiliers in AUCHY RIGHT. We have one company 2/5th Royal Warwicks attached. They have two platoons with "C" Coy. and two platoons with "D" Coy. They are a second line Territorial battalion. The Cameronians are on our left and the 15th Div. on our right. Enemy very quiet. Weather brilliant and wind in the West.	
	4th.June,1916.		Enemy very quiet. A few shells landed in the neighbourhood of High Street causing no material damage. Saps are being dug under the parapet right out through our wire. These are well in hand. It is proposed to have one per platoon as jumping off places. The C.O. and Officers of 2/5th. Warwicks visited the trenches and arranged the relief. One company of theirs is with us, another comes from the Cameronians and the remaining two from BEUVRY. We are to leave two companies in the village line in support of their battalion, together with our Specialist Officers and a few Signallers, Snipers, etc. The Cameronians on our left, raided the hostile trenches at 11 p.m. covered by a barrage of trench mortar and artillery fire. Results are not yet known. There was an absence of hostile rifle fire during the raid, which probably points to its having been swift and successful.	
	5th.June,1916.		Battalion was relieved by 2/5th. Royal Warwickshire Regiment, less two companies, which remained in reserve in the village line. Major Kennedy remained in command of these two companies. The two companies relieved were billeted in BEUVRY near Headquarters. One Officer and four N.C.O.'s were left behind attached to the 2/5th. Warwicks for their instruction, together with all the Specialist Officers of the battalion.	
	6th.June,1916.		Draft of 82 other ranks arrived from the 3/5th. Scottish Rifles, bringing the battalion well over strength. We have at the moment 41 Officers. The draft	

WAR DIARY

INTELLIGENCE SUMMARY

(Erase heading not required.)

Army Form C. 2118.

Instructions regarding War Diaries and Intelligence Summaries are contained in F. S. Regs., Part II. and the Staff Manual respectively. Title pages will be prepared in manuscript.

Place	Date	Hour	Summary of Events and Information	Remarks and references to Appendices
	6th.June,1916. (contd).		was complete in equipment but deficient in iron rations. These were made up from the Quartermaster's Store. It seems evident that the arrangements for the issue of iron rations at the Base are defective, as on several occasions drafts have arrived short of these rations.	
	7th.June,1916.		Commanding Officer inspected the draft in billets. It is reported that Lord Kitchener has been drowned on H.M.S. "Hampshire". At 11.30 p.m. a test Gas Alarm was carried out. The half battalion at BEUVRY had turned in for the night and most of the men were asleep. Time taken to get helmets adjusted - five minutes; and time taken until all had stood to - twenty minutes.	
	8th.June,1916.		At 3 p.m. the half battalion at BEUVRY moved to Jardins des Sports, BETHUNE, and were joined about 1 a.m. the following morning by the half battalion from the trenches. Troops were in bivouacs and much crowded. Ground was very wet and muddy and most uncomfortable.	
	9th.June,1916.		The battalion paraded in the Jardins des Sports. Owing to lack of space, and the heavy nature of the ground through rain, drill movements were much hampered. Orders received to move into BETHUNE tomorrow.	
	10th.June,1916.		The battalion moved to Montmorency Barracks, BETHUNE, at 5 p.m. We furnished Brigade Headquarters guard. Billets are good and have been treated with distemper, rendering them fresh and clean. Rifle racks are being put up in all the rooms by our Pioneers.	
	11th.to 16th. June,1916.		Training carried out on a large flat field which takes in the whole battalion. Strict attention is being paid to close order drill and handling of arms. All web equipment has been washed and buttons polished. On 13th.inst. all ranks were put through a chamber containing Chlorine gas. It was found that the P.H. helmet was a perfect safeguard and that no sensation of discomfort was experienced by our men. After coming out of the gas, tube helmets were taken off, and men allowed to breathe in one mouthful of the gas in order to satisfy them as to its strength and the impossibility of living in it without a helmet. Lewis Gun, Bayonet Fighting, Trench Mortar and Grenade courses	

Army Form C. 2118.

WAR DIARY
~~INTELLIGENCE SUMMARY~~
(Erase heading not required.)

Instructions regarding War Diaries and Intelligence Summaries are contained in F. S. Regs., Part II. and the Staff Manual respectively. Title pages will be prepared in manuscript.

Hour, Date, Place	Summary of Events and Information	Remarks and references to Appendices
11th. to 16th. June, 1916. (contd.)	are being attended by our men. Battalions to be inspected by the Corps Commander, General Haking, on the 17th. inst.	
17th. June, 1916.	Lieut.General Sir Robert Haking, accompanied by Major General Landon and Brigadier General Robertson, inspected the Battalion in the Jardins des Sport, ANNEZIN. The General spoke to a number of the men individually, and was pleased with their appearance. The A.D.M.S. later complimented the Commanding Officer on the appearance of the Battalion.	
18th. to 20th. June, 1916.	Battalion attended Church Parade in Opera House, BETHUNE, on Sunday morning. Four N.C.O's returned from Bayonet Fighting Class, all of whom were very well reported of for their work there. On the 20th. a Divisional Horse Show was held in BETHUNE. We had entries in four classes but secured no prizes. The Army Commander was present at the Horse Show.	
21st. June, 1916.	Battalion moved to billets in LE PREOL, where the usual working parties were carried on from day to day. Billeting area is very scattered but billets are good.	
22nd. June, 1916.	In the early morning, one of the largest mines ever put up on the Western front was blown at the Duck's Bill, by the Germans, and followed by one hour's intense bombardment of the front and support	

WAR DIARY

INTELLIGENCE SUMMARY.
(Erase heading not required.)

Army Form C. 2118.

Place	Date	Hour	Summary of Events and Information	Remarks and references to Appendices
	22nd June, 1916. (contd.)		lines. The enemy attacked with about 200 men and got into our trenches, but were very gallantly counter-attacked and driven out by the 2nd. Royal Welsh Fusiliers. A company of the Royal Welsh Fusiliers who had had most of the fighting was relieved by a company of the Cameronians, which in turn was relieved by "A" Company of Ours. Lieut. Stevenson, the Sapping Officer, was killed by a sniper while assisting in the consolidation of the crater. Lance-Corporal Erskine was successful in bringing in two wounded men, and very gallantly went out over the open and attended to Lieut. Stevenson, lying beside him until a shallow trench had been dug to the spot where he lay, whereby he was brought into the trenches.	
	23rd. June, 1916.		Our Artillery were active bombarding enemy's front line and communication trenches, and cutting wire.	
	24th. to 26th. June, 1916.		Artillery activity continues on the whole front. We are supplying working parties carrying bombs and consolidating the crater.	
	27th. June, 1916.		Battalion relieved 2nd. Royal Welsh Fusiliers in GIVENCHY LEFT SUB-SECTION, with four companies in the front line. The Cameronians are on our right and the 59th. Division on our left. Order of companies from left to right: "B", "D", "C", "A". During the night our artillery carried on a bombardment of the enemy's front and support lines, and constant sniping was kept up by the guns on gaps in the wire previously cut	
	28th. June, 1916.		About 7 a.m. on 28th. enemy exploded a mine in front of "C" Coy. about "F" sap, followed by a bombardment of the trenches. Our guns put up a heavy barrage and the enemy made no attempt to occupy the crater. Our trenches were blown in in parts, but working parties soon had them restored. During the day our guns were engaged cutting enemy's wire. There was a slight exchange of rifle grenades during the day. At 5 p.m. a large mine was blown by the enemy, about the same position as the one in the morning. Hostile artillery again bombarded the trenches, causing considerable damage, and our guns put up an effective barrage. No Infantry action followed. A patrol went out from the trench to the newly-	

Army Form C. 2118.

WAR DIARY
INTELLIGENCE SUMMARY.
(Erase heading not required.)

Place	Date	Hour	Summary of Events and Information	Remarks and references to Appendices
	28th. June, 1916. (contd.)		blown crater, and found it to be about 50 yards in diameter and 40 feet deep approximately. On the patrol's return it was sniped at by the enemy. Our men in "F" sap shot two Germans, and stopped the sniping. Sapping out to this crater was started at night.	
	29th. June, 1916.		Artillery was active generally, but, except for some wire cutting, no special bombardments were carried out. Rifle grenades were exchanged during the night. The trenches are in a very bad state owing to bad weather and the concussion from mine explosions. Large quantities of stores are being carried up nightly, and the work of rebuilding the trenches is being carried on. Some of the men are complaining of trench foot, and arrangements have been made for the washing of feet and the changing of socks. In spite of the fact that two mines have been exploded in the one day and that conditions are severe, all ranks are cheery and optimistic.

On the night of 29/30th. an attack and raid were done by the division on our left, while the Germans attacked the division on our right. Our operations were fairly successful, but the Germans were unable to reach our trenches. Guns continue sniping at gaps in the wire throughout the night. At 11 p.m. there was a special bombardment of the enemy trenches opposite our front. The enemy was very active with rifle grenades during the night, to which we replied heavily against their saps and front line. | |
| | 30th. June, 1916. | | The day was quiet. Two officers did a daylight patrol along the whole length of the Northern craters, from which much useful information was obtained. At 5 p.m. the enemy again blew a mine in front of "F" sap. This one is probably a surface mine, and beyond filling up a portion of "F" sap, did comparatively little damage. From the sap-head a view of the interior of the crater can be obtained. It is thought that the enemy is endeavouring to blow a line of craters right along his front as a defensive measure.

Summary:-

Strength on date: 40 Officers; 1067 Other Ranks. | |

Army Form C. 2118.

WAR DIARY

~~INTELLIGENCE SUMMARY~~

(*Erase heading not required.*)

Instructions regarding War Diaries and Intelligence Summaries are contained in F. S. Regs., Part II. and the Staff Manual respectively. Title pages will be prepared in manuscript.

Place	Date	Hour	Summary of Events and Information	Remarks and references to Appendices

	30th. June, 1916. (contd.)		Reinforcements during month: 81 Other Ranks, and 3 Officers from 6th. Scottish Rifles joined 10th. June.
			
			 Casualties:-
			     Killed: Officers - 1; Other Ranks - 3.
			     Wounded: Officers - 3; Other Ranks - 36.
			     Sick: Officers - 1; Other Ranks - 69.
				R Effrey Douglas Lt Col.
				 Comdg 5/6 Sco Rifles

19th Inf.Bde.
33rd Div.

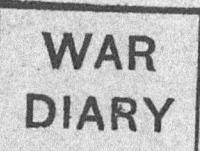

5th BATTN. THE CAMERONIANS (SCOTTISH RIFLES).

J U L Y

1 9 1 6

Attached:

Appendices I, II & III.

CONFIDENTIAL. 5TH. SCOTTISH RIFLES. July, 1916.

WAR DIARY
~~INTELLIGENCE SUMMARY~~
(Erase heading not required.)

Instructions regarding War Diaries and Intelligence Summaries are contained in F.S. Regs., Part II. and the Staff Manual respectively. Title pages will be prepared in manuscript.

Army Form C. 2118.

Hour, Date, Place	Summary of Events and Information	Remarks and references to Appendices
July 1st. to 3rd.	Battalion in trenches at GIVENCHY left. Artillery very active cutting wire opposite our front. Return by the enemy was weak. We have rifle grenade batteries of about 23 rifles in all, which have more or less silenced the rifle grenades of the enemy. Extensive patrolling is being done with a view to a raid on the enemy's trenches. It is reported that the enemy are mining under one of our saps, and in consequence the trenches for 50 yards on either side of this sap are held with the minimum garrison. On the morning of 3rd July about 10 a.m. Colonel Douglas was killed, being sniped in the head while in "B" sap. It is thought that he had been exposing his head over the papapet while observing with his periscope. Battalion was relieved by the 2nd. Royal Welsh Fusiliers on the evening of 3rd, and moved to billets in LE PREOL.	
July 4th.	Colonel Douglas was buried this afternoon in Bethune Cemetery, Grave No. 27, Band "T". Arrangements for the funeral were made by the 33rd Division. 2nd. Argyll & Sutherland Highlanders sent their pipers and buglers. Following senior officers were present:- General Landon, commanding 33rd. Division, and his Chief of Staff, General Robertson, commanding 19th. Brigade, and his Brigade Major, Colonel Chapman of the Cameronians, the Colonel of the 2nd. A.& S.H., Officer Commanding 19th. Field Ambulance, Major Stewart, Chaplain, and many others. Wreaths were sent by the 5th. Scottish Rifles, 2nd. Royal Welsh Fusiliers, and N.C.Os of 2nd. R.W.F. The six senior N.C.Os of the Battalion acted as pall-bearers, and were led by the pipers playing "Flowers of the Forrest". The Rev. John White conducted the funeral service. Major Kennedy assumed command of the Battalion today.	

Army Form C. 2118.

WAR DIARY
~~INTELLIGENCE SUMMARY~~

(Erase heading not required.)

Instructions regarding War Diaries and Intelligence Summaries are contained in F.S. Regs., Part II. and the Staff Manual respectively. Title pages will be prepared in manuscript.

Hour, Date, Place	Summary of Events and Information	Remarks and references to Appendices
July 5th.	Battalion reinforce 2nd. R.W.F. in GIVENCHY left, with two companies in front line, one in support and one in reserve. At 11.45 p.m. a raid was carried out on the German trenches by the 2nd. R.W.F. All objectives were gained. 43 prisoners taken, with two machine guns and a trench mortar. About 150 Germans killed. Our casualties were slight. As a diversion from the main raid, two parties of the 5th. Scottish Rifles made a bombing attack on the enemy sapheads and craters. This drew a considerable amount of the enemy's artillery fire, and fulfilled its object in creating a diversion. A few minor casualties were occasioned but only one wounded man was sent to hospital. On our right the 20th. Royal Fusiliers assisted operations by a gas demonstration, which was successful.	
July 6th.	There was no return by the enemy for last night's raid. Orders were received that the battalion was to be ready to move that night, as the 33rd. Division was being relieved. Kits were reduced to proper weight, transport packed up, and all surplus kits and material returned to central store for storage. Battalion was relieved by 4th/5th. Black Watch, and was billeted in Rue d'Aire, BETHUNE, on relief.	
July 7th.		
July 8th.	Orders received to entrain at FOUQUEREUIL Station at 6 p.m. Three hours were allowed for entrainment of transport and one hour and a quarter for Battalion. Entrainment was carried out speedily and train left at ten minutes to six.	
July 9th.	At 1.45 a.m. Battalion detrained at LONGUEAU, which is about two miles East of AMIENS, and marched to POULAINVILLE, a distance of about eight miles, arriving about 5 a.m. Billets are poor, and as the whole brigade is to be billeted in this small village there is very little accommodation for each battalion.	

Army Form C. 2118.

WAR DIARY
or
INTELLIGENCE SUMMARY.
(Erase heading not required.)

Instructions regarding War Diaries and Intelligence Summaries are contained in F. S. Regs. Part II. and the Staff Manual respectively. Title pages will be prepared in manuscript.

Place	Date	Hour	Summary of Events and Information	Remarks and references to Appendices
	July 10th.		We are now some miles behind ALBERT, just North of the SOMME, and are awaiting the completion of the Divisional move.	Appendix I. Confidential order by G.O.C. XI Army Corps.
	July 11th.		Moved from POULAINVILLE in the early morning to DAOURS where Battalion settled into Billets. Packs were withdrawn and stored.	
	July 12th.		Moved to BUIRE-SUR-L'ANCRE. Billeted there. This place appears to be a resting place for troops both coming up and going down the line. Large bodies of cavalry moving through.	
	July 13th.		Remained at BUIRE. Battalion on half hour's notice ready to move.	
	July 14th.		In the morning the Battalion marched to MEAULTE, and after having been billeted there about an hour moved on again in the direction of the trenches. The whole Brigade bivouacked in a field.n Just at dusk several shells were put into The Cameronians' lines, and in consequence the Brigade opened out.	See Appendix II maps.
	July 15th/16th.		The Brigade moved up at 4.30 a.m. Order of march:- The Cameronians, 5th. Scottish Rifles, 20th. Royal Fusiliers, 2nd. Royal Welsh Fusiliers. The morning was very misty and the air thick with gas from lachrymatory shells. The old front lines, British and German, were soon passed, and, after marching about two miles over the system of German trenches, the Brigade formed up behind the MAMETZ WOOD. The first attack order were received. The 98th. and 100th. Brigades were attacking the trench GERMAN SWITCH to the West of HIGH WOOD. When this was taken the 19th. was to push past them and take MARTINPUICH. The Brigade was expected to move about 9 a.m., but as the 98th. and 100th. Brigades were unable to gain their objective, the 19th. was not called out. In the afternoon the men dug themselves in, in holes, about the field. In the evening a large number of new gas shells were put over by the enemy. About 10 p.m. the Battalion moved off and dug themselves in on a line to the East of BAZENTIN-LE-PETIT, with one Company in support. A large number of casualties were suffered from first experience of poison gas shells.	

1577 Wt.W10791/1773 50,000 1/15 D.D.&L. A.D.S.S./Forms/C. 2118.

WAR DIARY of INTELLIGENCE SUMMARY.

(Erase heading not required.)

Army Form C. 2118.

Place	Date	Hour	Summary of Events and Information	Remarks and references to Appendices
	July 15th/16th (contd).		enfilading shrapnel, and in the morning the line was altered. The Germans were here about 700 yards away and out of view. The line occupied by the Battalion was from the CEMETERY to the WINDMILL, both East of BAZENTIN-LE-PETIT. The casualties for this day amounted to five officers and 65 other ranks. The wounded officers were: Captain A.G.Crombie, (remained on duty), Captain T.C.Smith, 2nd.Lieut. K.S.Miller, 2nd.Lieut. I.S.Donald and 2nd. Lieut. R.Wilson.	
	July 17th.		The same line was held. Casualties for this day were: 2nd.Lieut.W.S. Anderson and 30 other ranks. Late at night orders were given to dig in a sap post of 15 men to keep a new German work under observation, and harass them as much as possible. This was carried out.	
	July 18th.		The same positions were held. During the afternoon the left of the line was subjected to a heavy bombardment. In the evening the Battalion was relieved by the 20th. R.F. and returned to their former position at MAMETZ WOOD. The casualties for the day were: 2nd.Lieut. A.W.G.Smith and 2nd. Lieut. J.Cruikshanks wounded, five killed, and 46 other ranks wounded.	
	July 19th.		The Battalion remained at MAMETZ WOOD. In the evening orders were received for the 19th. Brigade to take HIGH WOOD.	See Appendix I Map.
	July 20th.		The Battalion left MAMETZ WOOD at 12.15 a.m., and marched by platoons on road past the BLASTED TREE, forming up on the road from BAZENTIN-LE-GRAND to MARTINPUICH, a little farther North than the cross-roads North of BAZENTIN-LE-GRAND. The bank of this road facing North-East had been trenched, and wire put out in front, but paths had been cut through this by the scouts, who were sent on in front to guide the Battalion through. This line was occupied by the 22nd. Manchesters. The Battalion then formed up in lines of sections in file facing HIGH WOOD, "C" Coy. on the right, "D" Coy. on the left, "A" in support, "B" in reserve, the 20th. Royal Fusiliers supporting in rear, and the 2nd. Royal Welsh Fusiliers in reserve. The Cameronians were on the left, attacking in the same line.	

WAR DIARY
INTELLIGENCE SUMMARY.
(Erase heading not required.)

Army Form C. 2118.

Place	Date	Hour	Summary of Events and Information	Remarks and references to Appendices
	July 20th. (contd)		The lines of sections then advanced, being preceded by the scouts. Our shelling was fairly light at first, but as time went on it intensified, until a tremendous bombardment was directed on the wood. The Germans replied by shrapnel, but in the dark it was impossible to tell the effect of it. By the flashes of the shrapnel on the right the 2nd. Gordons could be seen advancing in lines, they being the left Battalion of the 7th. Division, attacking on our right. About 3.25 a.m. the Battalion had arrived about 50 yards from the wood and formed up ready for the assault, keeping in the same formation. At 3.35 the guns being due to lift the assault was made, and the sections rushed through the wood, reached the farther side, and commenced to dig in. The opposition encountered consisted of some machine gun teams which were put out of action, and parties of Germans near dug-outs. One of these was bombed and in others about 30 prisoners were taken. There was a field gun emplacement in the right part of the wood with a fire burning among ammunition cases, but no signs of the gun could be seen. The Battalion was now mixed up with the 20th. Royal Fusiliers and a good number of the Cameronians who had appeared on the right, but the men were put under the nearest officers or N.C.Os. About 6 a.m. a heavy German bombardment commenced, a barrage being put up behind the wood. About 11 a.m. the Germans counter-attacked on the left through GERMAN SWITCH. The troops on the left fell back in considerable disorder, and this began to extend towards the right. They were however rallied in a trench across the middle of the wood by Major Macalister. He reformed them, and, after reconnaissance, pushed back again to the far side of the wood, where he was killed. The 2nd. R.W.F. now arrived, formed up on the road on the South-East side of the wood, and, forming up in lines of platoons, made a drive up it in a North-Westerly direction, clearing the wood. Some difficulty was experienced on the North-West side from machine guns and snipers, but they were eventually cleared, and the entire wood was held by the Brigade. About 9 p.m. a very heavy bombardment was opened on the wood by heavies, under cover of which a second counter-attack was made on the left. As the strength of the Brigade was now a mere handfull, the Germans obtained a footing, but the Southern and Eastern sides remained in our hands. After the bombardment was over,	

Army Form C. 2118.

WAR DIARY
or
INTELLIGENCE SUMMARY.
(Erase heading not required.)

Instructions regarding War Diaries and Intelligence Summaries are contained in F. S. Regs., Part II. and the Staff Manual respectively. Title pages will be prepared in manuscript.

Place	Date	Hour	Summary of Events and Information	Remarks and references to Appendices
	July 20th.(contd).		about 11 p.m. the Brigade was relieved, and what was left of the Battalion returned to MAMETZ WOOD. This amounted to one officer, and 198 other ranks. The officer casualties were	
			Lt.Col. A.A.Kennedy D.S.O., wounded,	
			Major W.C.Macallister, killed,	
			Capt. A.C.Crombie, wounded,	
			" W.S.Alexander, "	
			Lieut. D. Sinclair, "	
			" T.P.Spens, "	
			2/Lieut.R.L.Mitchell, "	
			" A.Hemilton, "	
			" B.G.Ashby, "	
			" J.A.Frew, "	
			" M.C.Wilson, "	
			" J. Phillips, "	
			" A.H.Laing, "	
			" W.F.Adam, "	
			" W.F.Brown, "	
			" G.G.Dalziel, died of wounds,	
			" J.R.Laird, missing.	
			" R.N.Johnston, "	
			There were 19 other ranks killed, 217 other ranks missing, 153 other ranks wounded.	
	July 21st.		Battalion rested behind MAMETZ WOOD. In the afternoon the Battalion moved back to BUIRE, Captain Munro, who had been Town-Major at MEAULTE, taking over command temporarily.	
	July 22nd.		Remained at BUIRE, Major H.C.Hyde Smith of The Cameronians taking over temporary command.	

Army Form C. 2118.

Instructions regarding War Diaries and Intelligence Summaries are contained in F.S. Regs., Part II. and the Staff Manual respectively. Title pages will be prepared in manuscript.

WAR DIARY
or
INTELLIGENCE SUMMARY.
(Erase heading not required.)

Place	Date	Hour	Summary of Events and Information	Remarks and references to Appendices
	July 23rd.		A draft of 394 other ranks belonging to the 5th., 6th., 8th. and 9th. Royal Scots arrived, and were posted to companies.	Appendix III Complimentary order by G.O.C. 33rd Division.
	July 24th.		Major E.R.Clayton D.S.O., late of the Staff of the XIth. Corps, took over command of the Battalion. Time was spent re-organising companies, training specialists, etc. A draft consisting of one warrant officer and 12 N.C.Os. of the 6th. Scottish Rifles, arrived today, and were posted to companies.	
	July 25th/29th.		Work at re-organising was carried on. Lewis Gunners, Bombers and Signallers courses were recommenced. Shortages in equipment, clothing and ordnance were made up. Some new N.C.Os appointed.	
	July 30th.		The Brigade was paraded in the afternoon and ribbons for the MILITARY MEDALS won in the recent fighting were distributed by Major-General H.J.S.Landon C.B., Divisional Commander. The following of the Battalion received the ribbon:- No. 6292, Sergt. A. E. Slade, No. 6721, L/Cpl. W. Gilchrist, No. 6823, Pte. J. McManus, No. 6432, Pte. J.J.N.Macfarlane.	

	July 31st.		The Battalion was inspected by Brigadier-General C.R. Mayne D.S.O., at 7.15 a.m. The Battalion formed up in mass, transport in rear. Training was continued during the remainder of the day.
			
			Strength at July 31st. - 18 Officers; 895 other ranks.
			
			Casualties during month:-
			
			Officers:- Killed - 3
			                Wounded - 22
			                Missing - 1
			                Sick - 1	

WAR DIARY or INTELLIGENCE SUMMARY.

Army Form C. 2118.

(Erase heading not required.)

Place	Date	Hour	Summary of Events and Information	Remarks and references to Appendices
	July 31st. (contd)		Other Ranks:- Killed - 27 Died of wounds - 4 Wounded - 266 Missing - 217 Sick - 35 E.R. Clayton Major, Commanding 5th. Scottish Rifles.	

A P P E N D I C E S   I, II & III.

5th. Scottish Rifles War Diary, July 1916. Appendix I.

(C O P Y)

All.
33rd.Div.

XI Corps.R.H.S.1137.

G.O.C.,
      33rd. Division.

    I wish you to convey to all ranks in your Division my great appreciation of the successful operations they have carried out during the time they have been in the Corps, operations which have received frequently the approbation of the General Officer Commanding the First Army, and of the Commander-in-Chief.

    The many raids that have been undertaken by the 33rd. Division have furnished models for other Divisions, newly arrived from England to join the Corps, and the two recently carried out by the GLASGOW HIGHLANDERS and the ROYAL WELSH FUSILIERS respectively have shown a brilliance in design and gallantry in execution which could not be surpassed.

    I have to thank all ranks for the ready response that they have made whenever I have called upon them to undertake any offensive operations. I have found a fine fighting spirit throughout the Division at all times, and it is with the greatest regret that I have to say "Good-bye".

    I have seen and spoken to nearly all the officers, and to many of the N.C.Os. and men of the Division, and I shall regret your departure more than that of any of the sixteen Divisions that have been in my Corps since it was formed, because you are all such fine fighting soldiers.

    I wish you "God speed and Victory", and I hope before the end of the war that I may again have the high honour of including the 33rd. Division in the XIth Corps under my Command.

                         (Signed) R. Haking, Lieut.Genl.,
                              Commanding XIth. Corps.

8th. July 1916.

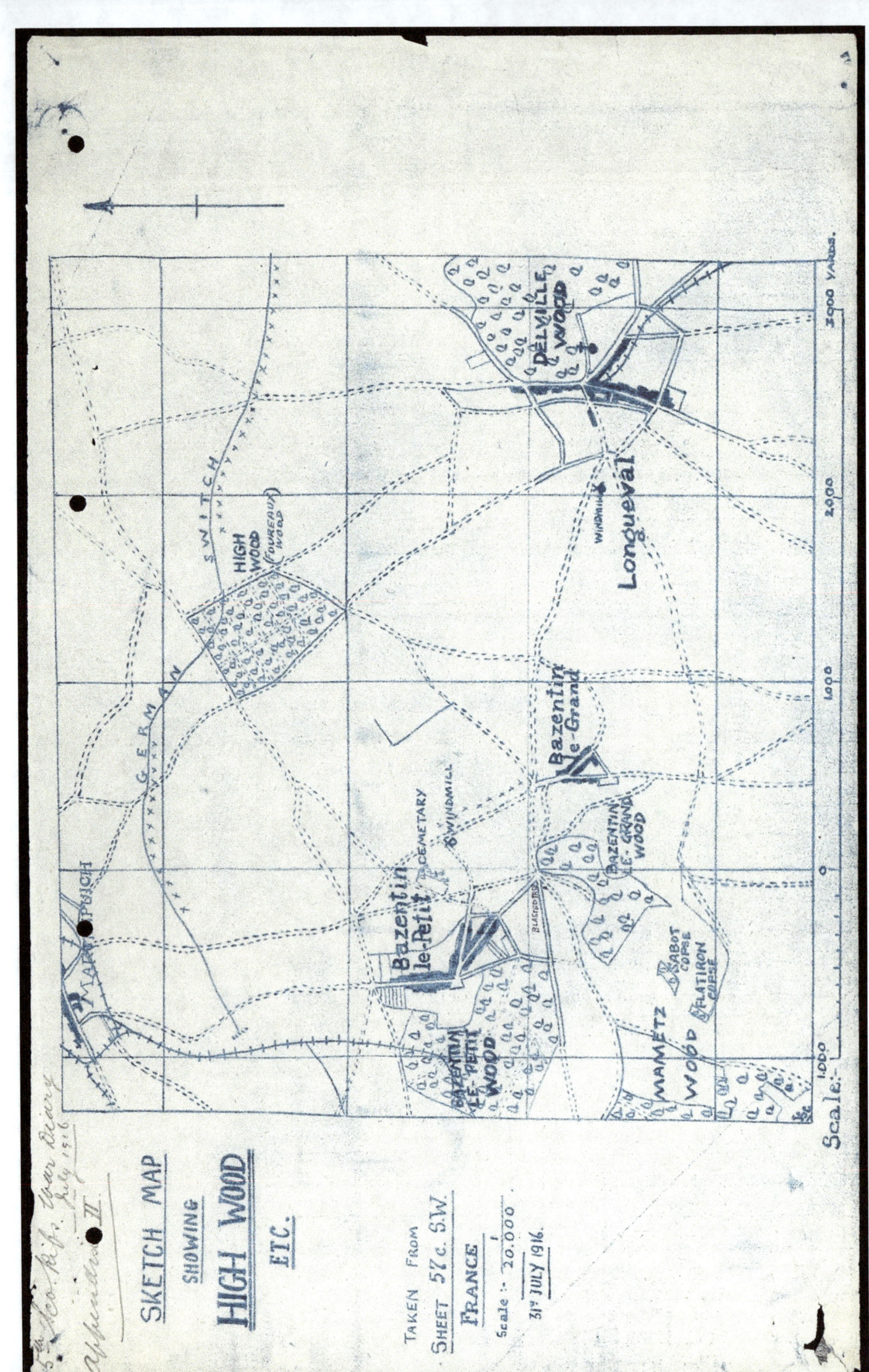

5th. Scottish Rifles War Diary, July 1916.   Appendix III.

(C O P Y)

19th. Brigade.

    The behaviour of the whole Division throughout the operations they have recently been engaged in has been worthy of their reputation.

    In the face of a series of most severe bombardments and in spite of heavy losses the Division most gallantly carried and held the objective of their second attack, the seizure of which will have a great effect on the success of further operations.

    My admirations and pride at the splendid spirit shown under most trying and difficult circumstances is unbounded.

    In feel confident in the abiltity and readiness, after a period of re-organization to continue active operations.

                                  (Signed) H.J.S.Landon, Major-Genl.,
                                           Commanding 33rd. Division.

23rd. July 1916.

19th Brigade
33rd Division.

1/5th BATTALION

SCOTTISH RIFLES

AUGUST 1916

CONFIDENTIAL.

5TH SCOTTISH RIFLES.
WAR DIARY
or
INTELLIGENCE SUMMARY.
(Erase heading not required.)

Army Form C. 2118.

AUGUST, 1916.

1/5 Scottish Rifles

Vol 22

Place	Date	Hour	Summary of Events and Information	Remarks and references to Appendices
	August 1/5th.		Training was carried on at BUIRE SUR L'ANCRE and progress began to be seen. Particular attention was paid to making the men mechanically take out their entrenching tools and dig themselves in. Advancing in lines of columns was steadily worked at. The Lewis Gun teams with reserves were put through a thorough course. A squad of 20 reserve bombers were trained, and signallers were started.	
	August 6th.		The Brigade moved to bivouacs between MEAULTE and BECORDEL, taking over from the 51st. Division.	
	August 7/12th.		The Battalion - less working parties - continued training on the same lines while in bivouacs.	
	August 13th.		Battalion moved to bivouacs in old German trenches on the edge of FRICOURT WOOD, one company being in FRICOURT VILLAGE. The ground was taken over from the 4th. Suffolks, who moved up to trenches.	
	August 13th./17th.		The men of the Battalion were mostly taken up for working parties, repairing roads, digging communication trenches, etc.	
	August 18th.		An attack was made by 98th. Brigade on WOOD LANE, a German trench S.E. of HIGH WOOD, the 19th. Brigade being in support. (See Appendix I.) Operation Orders. The Battalion was ordered to move at 6 p.m. and marched to trenches near CRUCIFIX CORNER, North of BAZENTIN-LE-GRAND, near the place where the attack on 20th. July was launched.	B.M.
	August 19th./20th.		Early in the morning the Battalion was ordered to take over from the 4th. Suffolks and 20th. Royal Fusiliers. The Cameronians taking over from the 4th. King's on our right, and the 2nd. Royal Welsh Fusiliers being in HIGH WOOD on our left. Later on, the Fusili took over from the Cameronians, making it a two battalion front. A great change had come over the place since being there last. Communication trenches were dug up to HIGH WOOD and the trenches on either side, and continual sapping forward was being carried out in the front line, to	

Army Form C. 2118.

WAR DIARY
INTELLIGENCE SUMMARY.
(Erase heading not required.)

Instructions regarding War Diaries and Intelligence Summaries are contained in F. S. Regs., Part II. and the Staff Manual respectively. Title pages will be prepared in manuscript.

Place	Date	Hour	Summary of Events and Information	Remarks and references to Appendices
	August 21st.		link up trenches on either side and get forward to the enemy. This sapping was pushed forward by the Battalion, wire was put up, and the ground in front patrolled. An attack was taking place on our right, about DELVILLE WOOD, and in order to spread out the area for enemy's retaliation smoke bombs were put off along the line to half way along our front. This, however, did not immediately affect us as it was done under the direction of the R.E., and the bombs thrown by bombers of the 20th. Royal Fusiliers. The 100th. Brigade made an attack on WOOD LANE on our right. Two companies of 20th. Royal Fusiliers were put in on our right, ready to take over trenches taken by the 100th. Brigade. (See Appendix I.) This order was afterwards cancelled, and the two companies remained in our trenches till the relief.	
	August 22nd.		The Battalion was relieved by the 20th. Royal Fusiliers and took over their bivouacs in the MAMETZ WOOD. Casualties for the tour of trenches were:- 1 Officer wounded (2/Lt.C.Rocks) 18 Other ranks killed, 55 Other Ranks wounded.	
	August 23rd.		While in MAMETZ WOOD working parties were supplied daily.	
	August 24th.		An attack was made by XIVth., XVth. and IIIrd. Corps in conjunction with the French simultaneously from the SOMME to MAUREPAS. The 100th. Brigade took part for the 33rd. Division. (See Appendix I.) Two companies of the 20th. Royal Fusiliers were in readiness to occupy trenches taken by the 100th. Brigade. Two companies ("B" and "D") of the 5th. Scottish Rifles went up to be attached to the 20th. Royal Fusiliers. The attack was successful, TEA TRENCH being captured.	
	August 25th.		The two remaining companies supplied working parties, carrying trench mortar ammunition and supplying mining fatigues. During our stay the Wood was subjected to considerable shelling. During this day 2/Lts.	

Army Form C. 2118.

WAR DIARY
~~INTELLIGENCE SUMMARY.~~
(Erase heading not required.)

Instructions regarding War Diaries and Intelligence Summaries are contained in F.S. Regs., Part II. and the Staff Manual respectively. Title pages will be prepared in manuscript.

Hour, Date, Place	Summary of Events and Information	Remarks and references to Appendices
August 26th.	Adam and Riddell were killed, and the Medical Officer, Captain T.C. Houston was fatally wounded, dying that night.	
	The two companies in MAMETZ WOOD moved up, taking over again from the 20th. Royal Fusiliers in the same trenches at 5 a.m. The principal piece of work was joining up the right of our front line WORCESTER TRENCH with the part of WOOD LANE newly taken. The four sapping platoons of the brigade were attached to the Battalion, and the work was completed, forming a new firing line, ready for a further advance.	
August 27th.	At 6 p.m. the Battalion was relieved by the 1st. Cameron Highlanders, 1st. Brigade, 1st. Division. They took over three companies. The 2nd. Argyll & Sutherland Highlanders, 98th. Brigade, took over from the right company and the Battalion returned to its former bivouacs in FRICOURT WOOD.	
August 28th.	The Battalion remained in FRICOURT WOOD and cleaned up generally, baths being provided.	
August 29th.	The Battalion moved to POMMIERS REDOUBT, taking over from The Cameronians. Working parties were supplied during the night. These had a very stiff time, a heavy thunderstorm coming on. There were also several casualties from machine gun fire.	
August 30th.	The Battalion moved back to the former bivouacing ground near MEAULTE.	
August 31st.	The Battalion moved back to RIBEMONT, and received orders to move farther back on the following day.	

Army Form C. 2118.

WAR DIARY

INTELLIGENCE SUMMARY.

(Erase heading not required.)

Instructions regarding War Diaries and Intelligence Summaries are contained in F. S. Regs., Part II. and the Staff Manual respectively. Title pages will be prepared in manuscript.

Hour, Date, Place	Summary of Events and Information	Remarks and references to Appendices
	Casualties for month were:-	
	Officers:- 2/Lt.W.T.Adam) Killed in action.	
	2/Lt.R.A.Riddell)	
	Captain T.C.Houston - died of wounds.	
	2/Lt. C. Rocks - wounded.	
	2/Lt.J.I.Scott - " .	
	Other Ranks:- Killed - 26	
	Wounded - 94	
	Missing - 4	
	Sick - 40	
	Reinforcements received:-	
	Officers - 26	
	Other Ranks -104.	
	Total strength of Battalion at date - 35 Officers.	
	795 Other ranks.	
	T.R.Clayhut. Col.,	
	Commanding 5th. Scottish Rifles.	

5th S.R. WAR DIARY AUGUST 1916.
APPENDIX No. 1.

SECRET.   Copy No. 3

19th Infantry Brigade - ORDER No.129.

Reference Map
LONGUEVAL 1/10,000.

                                                    23rd August 1916.

1. (a) The XIVth, XVth and III Corps are renewing the attack
      to-morrow.
   (b) The French are attacking simultaneously from the
       SOMME to MAUREPAS.

2. (a) The 100th Infantry Brigade, to which will be attached
       one battalion of the 98th Infantry Brigade, will capture
       and consolidate TEA TRENCH and the new German trench running
       from S.12.c.1.9. to S.11.a.3.3., and will connect up with the
       14th Division at S.12.a.55.30. It will then at once establish
       strong posts about S.12.a.55.30., in TEA
       LANE about S.12.a.00.55., in WOOD LANE about S.11.a.3.3., and
       also towards the enemy's main line between those points as
       necessary.

   (b) The attack will be carried out one hour after ZERO by
       the 2nd Worcesters, 16th K.R.R and 1st Queens with the
       9th H.L.I. in Reserve.

3. The attack will be preceded by a bombardment by Heavy
   Artillery starting at two hours before ZERO on the objectives
   to be attacked

4. In the event of the 100th Infantry Brigade gaining ground
   in WOOD LANE, the 19th Infantry Brigade will be prepared to
   take it over.
      For this purposes, two Companies of the 20th Royal
   Fusiliers, at present in the right subsection, will be concentrated
   about ST.GEORGES AVENUE, and held in readiness to move at once.

5. The Officer Commanding, 20th Royal Fusiliers will arrange to
   reconnoitre the way to WOOD LANE via DORSET TRENCH, and will
   have guides with each Platoon, who know their way from the top
   of ST. GEORGES AVENUE, to WOOD LANE via DORSET TRENCH.

6. (a) The 1st Queens will fire Very Lights to indicate the
       farthest point up WOOD LANE REACHED.
   (b) The 20th Royal Fusiliers will send one Officer with one
       Orderly to the Headquarters of the 1st Queens, 2½ hours before
       ZERO, who will, on the request of the Officer Commanding 1st
       Queens, immediately send for that portion of the two Companies
       of the 20th Royal Fusiliers required to hold the new line.

7. (a) Weather permitting 2 contact aeroplanes will be in the air
       from ZERO until 1 hour 30 minutes after ZERO. After that one
       contact aeroplane will be up until dark and from 5.30 a.m.
       to 7.30 a.m. on 25th August.

   (b) The Infantry in the front line will light flares.
       (i) On attaining the objective.
       (ii) At 7.30 p.m. on 24th August.
       (iii) At 6 a.m. 25th August.
       (iv) By 14th Division on reaching North Edge of DELVILLE WOOD.

   (c) Red flares will be used.

   (d) Each platoon of the two Companies of the 20th Royal Fusiliers
       will take with them ten flares, and will light them at the
       above hours, if they have taken over from the 100th Infantry
       Brigade.
          Any platoon which is not called upon, will return the
       flares to Battalion Headquarters.

- 2 -

8. (a) The new line taken over from the 100th Infantry Brigade will be at once consolidated, covering parties being pushed well forward into shell holes.
(b) A communication trench will be commenced back from WOOD LANE to our present line as soon as possible.
(c) The Sapping Platoon of the 1st Cameronians will report to the Officer Commanding 20th Royal Fusiliers, 2½ hours before ZERO and will be ready to commence digging out from our present line to meet the trench mentioned in para. (&).
(d) One Section of the 11th Company R.E. will be held in readiness at their bivouac to move up at once to WOOD LANE and form a strong point at the furthest point reached.

9. In order to allow the 20th Royal Fusiliers to concentrate two Companies, two Companies of the 1/5th Scottish Rifles will move up before daylight on the 24th instant, and take over part of the right Subsection. These Companies will come under the orders of the Officer Commanding 20th Royal Fusiliers.

10. Captain BETTS will place a smoke barrage with Stokes Mortars if the wind is favourable opposite the German Trench running from HIGH WOOD about S.4.d.2.7. towards S.4.d.5.7., and about the strong point at the East Corner of HIGH WOOD S.4.d.2.8. The smoke barrage will commence at 53 minutes after ZERO and be continued for 20 minutes.

11. Instructions for the cooperation of the 19th Machine Gun Company and 19th Trench Mortar Battery will be issued later.

12. Brigade Headquarters will remain at the QUARRY S.19.d.4.0.

Immediately the Companies of the 20th Royal Fusiliers move off, a report will be sent to Brigade Headquarters, and frequent reports of the situation will be sent in afterwards.

           Major.
          Brigade Major.
        19th Infantry Brigade.

Issued at 9.15 p.m.

    Copy No.1.2nd Royal Welsh Fus:
       2.1st Cameronians.
       3.1/5th Scottish Rifles.
       4.20th Royal Fusiliers.
       5.19th Machine Gun Coy.
       6.19th T.M.Bty.
       7.33rd Division (G).
       8.98th Infy.Bde.
       9.100th Infy.Bde.
      10.11th Coy. R.E.
      11.Staff Captain.
      12.Signals.
      13.Office.
      14.File.
      15.War Diary.

CONFIDENTIAL.

5TH. SCOTTISH RIFLES. September, 1916

WAR DIARY
or
INTELLIGENCE SUMMARY

(Erase heading not required.)

Army Form C. 2118.

Instructions regarding War Diaries and Intelligence Summaries are contained in F.S. Regs., Part II. and the Staff Manual respectively. Title pages will be prepared in manuscript.

Hour, Date, Place	Summary of Events and Information	Remarks and references to Appendices
September, 1st.	The Battalion moved from RIBEMONT, moving first along the ALBERT-AMIENS Road, then, branching off, moved along a second class road through several small villages. Dinners were issued at a halt after half-way. The destination was PIERREGOT, a small place about 14 km. North-East of AMIENS.	
September, 2nd.	The Battalion moved off at 8.30 a.m. The route was through TALMAS on the AMIENS-DOULLENS Road. A halt was again made after half-way and dinner taken. The route in the afternoon was through CANDAS - Army Headquarters of R.F.C. - then through FIENVILLERS to AUTHEUX, where the Battalion billeted.	
September, 3rd.	The Battalion rested in billets.	
September, 4th.	The Battalion moved through LE MEILLARD, FROHEN-LE-PETIT, and FROHEN-LE-GRAND to BONNIERES. This was a rather better village than those we had been accustomed to of late. As well as the 5th. Scottish Rifles, the 2nd. Royal Welsh Fusiliers and 20th. Royal Fusiliers were in the same village.	
September, 5th.	The Brigade moved thru' VACQUERIE, MONCHEL, BLANGERMONT, and the Battalion billeted in LINZEUX.	
September, 6th.	There was a short move to HERICOURT, a small place about 9 km. South-West of ST POL.	
September, 7th.	The Brigade did not move.	
September, 8th.	The Battalion moved by HAUTE-COTE, NUNCQ, and billeted in HOUVIN-HOUVIGNEUL. This village was considerably cleaner and better than most, and there was plenty of accommodation.	
September, 9th.	This day's move was by REBREUVIETTE to IVERGNY, a small place	

WAR DIARY
INTELLIGENCE SUMMARY.
(Erase heading not required.)

Army Form C. 2118.

Instructions regarding War Diaries and Intelligence Summaries are contained in F.S. Regs., Part II. and the Staff Manual respectively. Title pages will be prepared in manuscript.

Hour, Date, Place	Summary of Events and Information	Remarks and references to Appendices
September, 9th.(contd.)	about 10 km. North of DOULLENS.	
September, 10th.	A further move South-West was made, which brought the Battalion to POMMIER, its destination in the new area. The first part of the march was through the FORET-de-LUCHEUX; then, passing LUCHEUX; HUMBERCOURT; COULLEMONT the ARRAS-DOULLENS Road was crossed, and the destination reached. At the halt for dinner the General Officer Commanding the VIIth. Army Corps - to which the Division now belonged - Lieut.-General Sir T.D'O.A. Snow, walked round the Battalion. POMMIER is a small village with nothing of interest in it. Although only about 2½ miles from the trenches it is practically untouched by shells. It is almost exactly half-way between ARRAS and DOULLENS, though about 3 miles South-West of half-way on the main road.	
September, 11th/14th.	Training was continued in fields around the village. The transport and quartermasters' stores of all the Division were together at LA BAZEQUE FARM, about three miles farther back. Company Officers reconnoitred the trenches, which were found to be very quiet, and in some places as far apart as 1500 yards.	
September, 15th.	The Battalion relieved the Cameronians in the evening, the trenches running from in front of FONQUEVILLERS towards HANNESCAMPS in our lines, being a little North of GOMMECOURT, which is in the German lines.	
September, 20th.	The Battalion was relieved at night by the Cameronians, and went to POMMIER. The spell in trenches was very quiet. Considerable patrolling was carried out and work done to trenches. The casualties were very slight; 2/Lt. T.H.Haddow wounded; two other ranks killed and two wounded.	

WAR DIARY
~~INTELLIGENCE SUMMARY~~

(Erase heading not required.)

Army Form C. 2118.

Instructions regarding War Diaries and Intelligence Summaries are contained in F.S. Regs., Part II. and the Staff Manual respectively. Title pages will be prepared in manuscript.

Hour, Date, Place	Summary of Events and Information	Remarks and references to Appendices
September, 21st.	Training continued at POMMIER.	
September, 22nd.	The Battalion moved to ST AMAND, another village, about two miles South-East of POMMIER, and became Divisional Reserve. The billets were rather better here than at POMMIER, the men being in huts, all together.	
September, 24th.	Another Battalion came into the village. It belonged to the WEST RIDING Division. Half of the camp was given up to them, one company being put into billets in the village.	
September, 26th.	The Battalion again relieved the Cameronians in the same sector. Orders were issued for a move back for training.	
September, 28th.	The Battalion was relieved by the 6th. West Riding Regiment, and on relief moved to HUMBERCAMP, a village two miles West of POMMIER.	
September, 29th.	The Battalion remained in HUMBERCAMP.	
September, 30th.	The Battalion moved back for training. The route was by PAS to the ARRAS - DOULLENS Road and straight in to the latter town, where the Battalion - along with the 20th. Royal Fusiliers, was billeted. The distance was about 12 miles. DOULLENS is a fair sized town with population between 4/5000. The billets for troops were not particularly good, and were scattered. Instructions regarding training were issued. Strength of Battalion at date:- 44 officers; 968 other ranks. Casualties during month:- 2/Lt.J.H.Haddow wounded; 2/Lt.H.B. Robertson, transferred to England sick; 3 other ranks killed; 5 other ranks wounded; 123 other ranks to hospital sick.	

Army Form C. 2118.

WAR DIARY
or
INTELLIGENCE SUMMARY.
(Erase heading not required.)

Instructions regarding War Diaries and Intelligence Summaries are contained in F.S. Regs., Part II and the Staff Manual respectively. Title pages will be prepared in manuscript.

Hour, Date, Place	Summary of Events and Information	Remarks and references to Appendices

September, 30th. (contd.)	Reinforcements received:—
	
	     Captain H.B.Spens;
	   2/Lieut.W.D.Logen;
	       " J.McG.Maguire;
	       " W.McChlery;
	       " R.A.Carswell;
	       " J.McLachlan;
	       " F.Baird Smith;
	       " D.Muirhead;
	       " A.W.Mackinnon;
	       " R.M.Young;
	       " D.A.Rigby;
	
	 and 270 other ranks.
	
	                   SMClough Lt..Col.,
	           Commanding 5th. Scottish Rifles.	

CONFIDENTIAL.

Army Form C. 2118.

5TH. SCOTTISH RIFLES. OCTOBER, 1918.

WAR DIARY

INTELLIGENCE SUMMARY

(Erase heading not required.)

19/33

24.0 Sheets

Place	Date	Hour	Summary of Events and Information	Remarks and references to Appendices
	October 1st./9th.		The Battalion remained in DOULLENS. Training was continued pretty much on the same lines, the special features being advancing in lines of columns, and wood fighting. On 9th. a practice attack was carried out by the whole brigade on model trenches dug on North side of the Town, the trenches being a copy of the German trenches which would be the Brigade's next objective.	
	October 10th.		The Battalion left in the morning in motor buses for a wood North-East of IVERGNY, which resembled the wood to be attacked by The Cameronians and the 5th. Scottish Rifles. After the morning's work the Battalion returned to DOULLENS.	
	October 11th.		The Battalion moved back to the line, leaving DOULLENS in buses and reaching BAYENCOURT, where tents and bivouacs were put up.	
	October 12th./15th.		The Battalion remained in BAYENCOURT. BAYENCOURT. Working parties were supplied.	
	October 16th./17th.		The Battalion moved to trenches; 2) company in trenches, Battalion Headquarters and one company in HEBUTERNE, two companies in SAILLY-AU-BOIS. It was from here that the expected attack was to come off. Great preparations had been made; the country behind was full of guns and the enemy's wire was being cut. Stores of bombs and trench mortars were brought up, and preparations of all descriptions were being carried out.	
	October 18th		The Battalion was relieved by 7th. Yorks Regt. of the 17th. Division, and moved back to BAYENCOURT. It became known that the attack was not to take place at this part.	
	October 19th		The Battalion embussed at SOUASTRE and proceeded to DOULLENS.	
	October 20th.		The Battalion left DOULLENS at 1.30 p.m., embussed in French buses, and proceeded South to VILLE-SOUS-CORBIE, via AMIENS and BUIRE.	
	October 21st.		The Battalion remained at VILLE.	

Army Form C. 2118.

WAR DIARY
INTELLIGENCE SUMMARY
(Erase heading not required.)

Instructions regarding War Diaries and Intelligence Summaries are contained in F. S. Regs., Part II. and the Staff Manual respectively. Title Pages will be prepared in manuscript.

Place	Date	Hour	Summary of Events and Information	Remarks and references to Appendices
	October 22nd.		The Brigade moved East by MEAULTE, and took over a Camp - The CITADEL - South of FRICOURT.	
	October 23rd.		The Brigade moved by cross-country tracks past MONTAUBAN to BERNAFAY WOOD, beside which the Battalion bivouacked.	
	October 24th.		The Battalion moved to bivouacs and shelters beside GUILLEMONT, the Brigade being in support to the 4th. Division, which was attacking.	
	October 25th./26th.		The Brigade relieved the 11th. Infantry Brigade, 4th. Division, the 2nd. R.W.F. and 20th. R.F. being in the line in front of LES BOEUFS, THE 5th. Scottish Rifles in support behind LES BOEUFS and MORVAL, and The Cameronians in reserve at GUILLEMONT. The Brigade was now the right brigade of the XIVth. Army Corps, being now the right of the British line, joining with the French. The Trench 152nd. Division was on the right of the Brigade. While in these trenches working parties were supplied for the front line, and work was carried out in improving the defences of the line. As the trenches at present held were formerly German, they were altered to face the opposite direction and new wire put out.	
	October 27th.		The Battalion took over from the 20th. Royal Fusiliers, one company being in the front line, one in German gun pits, one in support immediately in front of LES BOEUFS, and one in reserve.	
	October 28th.		The 1st. Middlesex, of the 98th. Brigade, on the left, attacked at 6 a.m. and took the German trench (DEWDROP TRENCH) opposite them. The capture of this trench cut off a party of Germans in organised shell-holes in front of the company in the gun pits, and about two officers and about 30 of the enemy suddenly appeared shouting "KAMERAD". This statement, however, was doubted by most of the company in the gun pits, and they jumped on the parapet and prepared to decide the question by the bayonet. The Germans, seeing this, made for the Middlesex lines	

WAR DIARY
INTELLIGENCE SUMMARY

(Erase heading not required.)

Army Form C. 2118.

Place	Date	Hour	Summary of Events and Information	Remarks and references to Appendices
	October 28th. cortd.		and gave themselves up there. One prisoner unwounded was taken, and one wounded German brought in. They both belonged to the 15th. Bavarian Regt. Two German machine guns were captured in unoccupied gun pits. They were complete with ammunition and spare parts and were trained on our trenches. The second of these was captured by daylight shortly after the prisoners came over. ~~[struck through text]~~ Later in the day the men were all seen smoking cigars. These were traced to a German dug-out in the gun pits.	
	October 29th.		Orders were received for the front line company to attack the German trench opposite – HAZY TRENCH – in conjunction with The Cameronians on the right. (See Appendix). "D" Company attacked; "A" in support; at 5.45 a.m. Three platoons of "D" Company deployed on the parapet and assaulted slightly before The Cameronians. Immediately the men crossed the parapet, machine gun fire was opened on them by 3 or 4 machine guns. The guns were believed to be in shell-holes in advance of HAZY TRENCH. The result was that, after going about 50 yards, the attacking platoons were so much reduced in numbers that although some men got within 20 yards of the enemy's trench they were unable to effect anything. The remnants of the company lay down in NO MAN'S LAND unable to move. Captain D.D.Clarkson, in command of the company, seeing that the attack was not proceeding well, put in three sections of his reserve platoon. These men had hardly crossed the parapet when they were caught by machine gun fire. The whole attack was over in less than two minutes. Captain H.B.Spers, in command of "A" Company, which was now in the front line, seeing how things stood, decided to make no further attempt to advance an took over charge of the line. This was kept under by fire from our front men lying in NO MAN'S LAND. There was a great deal of machine gun and rifle fire directed on the	See appendix

Army Form C. 2118.

WAR DIARY
INTELLIGENCE SUMMARY

(Erase heading not required.)

Instructions regarding War Diaries and Intelligence Summaries are contained in F. S. Regs., Part II. and the Staff Manual respectively. Title Pages will be prepared in manuscript.

Place	Date	Hour	Summary of Events and Information	Remarks and references to Appendices

	October 29th contd.		line and Lewis guns.
			At night stretcher parties collected wounded; the unwounded and some wounded crawled in.
			The casualties for the attack were:-
			
			    2/Lt. J.A.B.Macharg) killed.
			    2/Lt. J.Macdonald)
			    26 other ranks killed.
			    34 other ranks wounded.	

	October 30th.		The Battalion was relieved by the 2nd. Worcestershire Regt, of the 100th. Brigade, and moved back to Camp near BERNAFAY WOOD. The relief was very slow, and owing to the thick mud, shell holes, and enemy's barrage the men arrived at the camp in a very exhausted state.	

	October 31st.		The Battalion moved to huts at CARNOY. These huts are situated just behind where the old British front line was. The old trenches - British and German - wire and mine craters are just at the edge of the Camp.
			
			Strength at date:-
			
			Casualties during the month:-
			    Captain J.M.Grierson, wounded.
			    2/Lt. J.A.B.Macharg, killed.
			    2/Lt. J.Macdonald, killed.
			
			    35 other ranks killed.
			    69 other ranks wounded.
			    9 other ranks missing.
			
			Reinforcements received during month:-	

Army Form C. 2118.

WAR DIARY
or
INTELLIGENCE SUMMARY
(Erase heading not required.)

Instructions regarding War Diaries and Intelligence Summaries are contained in F. S. Regs., Part II. and the Staff Manual respectively. Title Pages will be prepared in manuscript.

Place	Date	Hour	Summary of Events and Information	Remarks and references to Appendices
	October 31st. contd.		55 other ranks.	
			[signature] Lt.Col., Commanding 5th. Scottish Rifles.	

Appendix to War Diary Octr 1916.

(COPY)

S E C R E T.   Copy No. 4.

19TH. INFANTRY BRIGADE ORDER NO. 167.

Ref.Maps 57c.S.W. 1/20,000.
Situation Map X.A.3 1/10,000.   October 28th., 1916.

1. Order No. 166 is cancelled.

2. The 19th. Infantry Brigade will attack HAZY TRENCH tomorrow morning, but not BORITSKA.

3. The attack will be done with a rush at 5.45 a.m. tomorrow morning by The Cameronians and 5th. Scottish Rifles.

4. The objectives are as follows:-

(a) 1st.Cameronians. From junction of BORITSKA and HAZY TRENCHES to T.5.a.9.6, where HAZY TRENCH crosses the track.

(b) 5th. Scottish Rifles. From T.5.a.9.6 to Northern end of HAZY TRENCH.

On objectives being gained outposts will be pushed forward to the North and North-East.

5. There will be no artillery barrage before the attack.

(a) At 5.48 a.m. a stead Field Artillery barrage will open 150 yards East of HAZY TRENCH, and across BORITSKA TRENCH, 100 yards South-East of its junction with HAZY.

(b) The ground farther East will also be bombarded by our own artillery and that of the Divisions on the right and left.

6. Immediately HAZY TRENCH is captured the following will be carried out:-

(a) A block will be made at the junction of BORITSKA and HAZY TRENCHES by the 1st. Cameronians.

(b) A strong point will be made at the North End of HAZY TRENCH by the 5th. Scottish Rifles.

Commanding Officers will arrange for parties to be ready to dig forward from our present trenches.

7. A Brigade dump has been established near the right Battalion Headquarters in the SUNKEN ROAD T.4.d. Battalions will arrange to carry forward from here with their own

(2)

carrying parties any further stores required.

8. Prisoners will be sent to the cage at T.e. where they will be taken over by the A.P.M.

9. Stragglers' posts E. of LES BOEUFS will be arranged by Battalions.

The 20th. Royal Fusiliers will collect stragglers at OX TRENCH.

10. (a) Flares will be lit as soon as the objective is gained, and when called for by a contact aeroplane.

(b) Signalling flags will be carried and will be waved to show the Artillery the Infantry positions. On no account will flags be stuck in the ground.

11. Watches will be synchronised with Brigade Headquarters on receipt of this order.

Issued at 9 p.m.   (Signed) E.K.Twiss, Major,
Brigade Major,
19th. Inf. Brigade.

Copy No. 1. G.O.C.
2. 2nd. Royal Welsh Fusiliers.
3. 1st. Cameronians.
4. 5th. Scottish Rifles.
5. 20th. Royal Fusiliers.
6. 19th. Machine Gun Company.
7. 19th. Trench Mortar Battery.
8. 33rd. Division "G".
9.   do.   "Q".
10. 98th. Inf. Bde.
11. 100th. Inf. Bde.
12. Staff Captain.
13. Signals.
14. Supply Officer.
15. File.

(COPY) APPENDIX II.

War Diary October 1916

To "A" "D" Coy.

A.28/15.   28.

1. The Cameronians and "D" Coy. 5th. Sco. Rifles will capture and consolidate HAZY trench.

2. HAZY trench will be rushed at 5.45 a.m. tomorrow, October 29th.

Objectives are as follows:-

<u>Cameronians</u>. From junction of BORITSKA and HAZY trenches to T.5.a.9.6 AAA

<u>"D" Coy. 5/S.R.</u> From T.5.a.9.6, where HAZY trench crosses the track, to NORTHERN end of HAZY trench AAA

The Cameronians are advancing from FROSTY trench AAA

"D" Coy. 5th. Sco. Rifles will advance from its present position AAA

3. "A" Coy. will support the left flank of "D" Coy. and will be prepared to occupy "D" Coy's present line after the attack AAA

4. There will be no artillery barrage before the rush, but a barrage will be put on at 5.48 a.m., 200 yards behind HAZY trench, and will be kept on during consolidation AAA

"A" Coy. will furnish a party to dig forward a communication trench to HAZY Trench after capture AAA

5. A strong point will be made by "D" Coy. at the Northern end of HAZY trench immediately after capture AAA The junction of HAZY and BORITSKA trenches are being blocked by The Cameronians AAA

6. O.C. "A" Coy. will put any tools in his possession at the disposal of O.C. "D" Coy. AAA

7. Watches are to be corrected by a watch sent with orders AAA

8. Acknowledge AAA

From: 5/S.R.

Time: ~~1.50 a.m.~~

(Signed) J.S. Coltart, Lt. & A/Adjt.

CONFIDENTIAL.

5TH. SCOTTISH RIFLES.

WAR DIARY

INTELLIGENCE SUMMARY

(Erase heading not required.)

NOVEMBER, 1916.

Army Form C. 2118.

Vol 25

Place	Date	Hour	Summary of Events and Information	Remarks and references to Appendices
	Novr.1st./2nd.		The Battalion remained in huts at CARNOY. Work parties were supplied.	
	Novr.3rd.		The Brigade took over the line from the 98th. Brigade, the Battalion relieving the 4th. Suffolks in the FLERS line. Further working parties were provided.	See App.I.
	Novr.4th./5th.		An attack was arranged to take place on 5th. at 11 a.m. The 2nd. Royal Welch Fusiliers and 20th. Royal Fusiliers were in the line, The Cameronians and 5th. Scottish Rifles being Divisional Reserve. The Battalion moved to its former position in OX AND BOVRIL trenches during the night, being in position by daylight.	See App.II.
	Novr.5th.		The attack came off successfully on the Divisional front, an advance of about 1000 yards being made.	See App.III.
	Novr.5th./6th.		Immediately after dark the Battalion - which was attached to the 100th. Brigade - moved up to take over the newly gained trenches and to connect with the French left. Great difficulty was experienced in locating where the line had been taken up. During the relief some casualties were suffered owing to part of a relieving Company coming under hostile machine gun fire.	
	Novr.6th.		The 100th. Brigade was relieved by a Brigade of the 8th. Division. Careful arrangements for guides were made with the relieving Units, and the relief went off very quickly.	See App.IV.
	Novr.6th./7th.		On relief the Battalion occupied bivouacs at TRONES WOOD.	
	Novr.7th.		The Battalion moved back to the huts at CARNOY.	
	Novr.8th./10th.		The Brigade moved back to MEAULTE, and remained there until 11th.	

Army Form C. 2118.

WAR DIARY

INTELLIGENCE SUMMARY

(Erase heading not required.)

Instructions regarding War Diaries and Intelligence Summaries are contained in F. S. Regs., Part II. and the Staff Manual respectively. Title Pages will be prepared in manuscript.

Place	Date	Hour	Summary of Events and Information	Remarks and references to Appendices
	Novr.11th./16th.		The Division moved back to South of ABBEVILLE. The Battalion entrained at BUIRE in two trains at 12 noon and 2 p.m. and proceeded - by degrees, past AMIENS and LONGPRE to AIRAINES, where it detrained. The trains arrived at AIRAINES at 2.30 a.m. and 3.15 a.m. respectively. From here the Companies marched to billets in small villages - FRESNE-TILLOLOY and VAUX-MARQUENNEVILLE - where they arrived about 7.30 a.m. The Transport had gone by road the whole way, and was already at the billets. The Battalion commenced cleaning, refitting and training. Courses for specialists commenced. While the Battalion was quartered at FRESNE-TILLOLOY the son of the Mayor was buried. An Officer, 15 men and 4 pipers were sent to represent the Battalion.	
	Novr.17th./23rd.		The Battalion moved to ALLERY, where billets were a great improvement on FRESNE-TILLOLOY. Work was continued here on the same lines. Divisional Football League, Boxing Tournament and Concert parties were in full working order. The Regimental Canteen and Recreation Room opened, so that the spare time of the men was catered for.	

	Novr.24th. Novr.25th./30th.		The Battalion was inspected by Major-General PINNEY, G.O.C. 33rd.Division, Otherwise training on the same lines was continued until the end of the month.
			
			Casualties during month:-
			      Killed: 3 other ranks.
			      Wounded:19 do.
			      Missing:41 do.
			
			Reinforcements received:-
			      2/Lt. W.Barbour.
			      2/Lt. R.Downie.
			      2/Lt. J.Owen.
			      54 other ranks.	

Army Form C. 2118.

WAR DIARY

~~INTELLIGENCE SUMMARY~~

(Erase heading not required.)

Instructions regarding War Diaries and Intelligence Summaries are contained in F. S. Regs., Part II. and the Staff Manual respectively. Title Pages will be prepared in manuscript.

Place	Date	Hour	Summary of Events and Information	Remarks and references to Appendices
	Novr. 30th. contd.		Strength at date:- 38 officers: 776 other ranks.	
			EK Clayton Lt. Col., Commanding 5th. Scottish Rifles.	

2449 Wt. W14957/M90 750,000 1/16 J.B.C. & A. Forms/C.2118/12.

CONFIDENTIAL.

5TH SCOTTISH RIFLES.

WAR DIARY
or
INTELLIGENCE SUMMARY
(Erase heading not required.)

Army Form C. 2118.

DECEMBER, 1916.

Vol 26

Place	Date	Hour	Summary of Events and Information	Remarks and references to Appendices
	December 1st./6th.		The Battalion remained in ALLERY. Training continued on the same lines.	
	December 7th.		The Division commenced to move back to the forward area. The Battalion transport moved off, making the whole journey by road.	
	December 8th.		The Battalion entrained to AIRAINES at 7 a.m., and reached MERICOURT about 1 p.m., where it detrained and marched to huts, recently occupied by the French, at MORLANCOURT.	
	December 9th.		The Brigade, with transport, moved to huts about 1½ miles North of BRAY, and remained there the following day.	
	December 11th.		The Battalion moved to huts at North side of SUZANNE, where it became part of Divisional reserve. The Battalion remained here until the 14th. December. The Division was now once more the right British Division, joining with the French on the right and the 4th. Division on the left. It formed part of the XV Army Corps.	
	December 14th.		The Battalion moved into the line from SUZANNE, and relieved the 2nd. Worcestershire Regt. in trenches in front of RANCOURT and opposite the Southern end of ST.PIERRE-VAAST WOOD. The ground was exceptionally wet; there were no communication trenches; the way up was through a mixture of mud and shell holes; and the trenches when reached were broken-down and very wet. Apart from these hardships the trenches were very quiet; the Germans did very little sniping, and machine guns and artillery were inactive. There were two companies in the front line, one in support and one in reserve. The Battalion Headquarters was situated on the BETHUNE-PERONNE Road.	
	December 16th.		The two front line companies were relieved by the support and reserve companies and the dispositions altered to two companies in the front line and two in reserve. The physical conditions were made worse by the change in weather from rain to frost and snow, which caused some cases of	

WAR DIARY

~~INTELLIGENCE SUMMARY~~

(Erase heading not required.)

Army Form C. 2118.

Instructions regarding War Diaries and Intelligence Summaries are contained in F. S. Regs, Part II. and the Staff Manual respectively. Title Pages will be prepared in manuscript.

Place	Date	Hour	Summary of Events and Information	Remarks and references to Appendices
	December 16th.(contd).		trench feet. Though work was carried on, bailing out and clearing the trenches, they were still in a very bad state and great difficulty was encountered bring up rations, water and stores. Communication trenches were worked at however by the R.E. and Pioneer Battalion.	
	December 18th.		The Battalion was relieved at night by the 2nd.R.W.F. and moved back to a camp at MAUREPAS. While at MAUREPAS nothing of any consequence occurred. The valley and the vicinity of the camp received a certain amount of shelling. The Battalion only suffered one casualty; R.Q.M.S. McKnight, wounded.	
	December 22nd.		The Battalion was relieved by the 4th. Suffolks and took over the former huts North of SUZANNE.	
	December 26th.		The Battalion moved via BRAY to Camp 12, North of SAILLY-LAURETTE.	
	December 27th.		The Brigade entrained at EDGE HILL Station, near BUIRE, and detrained at PONT REMY, near ABBEVILLE. The journey took about four hours From PONT REMY the Battalion marched to BELLANCOURT, a distance of about 5 miles, where it was billeted.	
	December 31st.		Training commenced on the usual lines, and arrangements were made for opening the canteen, etc., also for a New Year dinner for the men. Casualties during the month:- Killed:- 3 other ranks. Wounded:- 15 do. Missing:- 3 do. Reinforcements received during the month:- 2/Lt. N. Clark. 2/Lt. A. T. Baillie	Warrant officers in the batt wanted commissions

WAR DIARY
~~or~~ INTELLIGENCE SUMMARY
(Erase heading not required.)

Army Form C. 2118.

Place	Date	Hour	Summary of Events and Information	Remarks and references to Appendices
	December 31st.(contd).		179 other ranks. Strength at end of month:- 41 officers. 876 other ranks.	

E.R. Clery/hn Lt. Col.,
Commanding 5th. Scottish Rifles.

CONFIDENTIAL.

Army Form C. 2118.

5TH SCOTTISH RIFLES.
WAR DIARY
or
INTELLIGENCE SUMMARY
(Erase heading not required.)

JANUARY, 1917.

Vol 27

27.C.
Sheet

Instructions regarding War Diaries and Intelligence Summaries are contained in F. S. Regs., Part II. and the Staff Manual respectively. Title Pages will be prepared in manuscript.

Place	Date	Hour	Summary of Events and Information	Remarks and references to Appendices
	January 1st./12th.		In the New Years' Honours List the following awards were made to this Battalion:- Military Cross Lt. T.P. Spens C.S.M.(now 2/Lt.) W. Barbour D.C.M. Mentioned in Despatches. Lt. Col., L.A. Clayton D.S.O. Major W.G. MacAlister (Killed) Sgt. (now 2/Lt.) A.T. Baillie No. 147 Cpl. J. Wilson The Battalion remained at BELLANCOURT. Training continued, each platoon working by itself. Lewis gunners and bombers were also trained and all deficiencies made up.	
	January 13th.		The Divisional Commander Major-General R.J. Pinney C.B. presented medal ribbons to certain officers and men who had been awarded them during the past six months. The awards were as follows:- No. 7064 Sgt. J. Erskine V.C. Capt. J.S. Coltart M.C. 2/Lt. L.C. Davies (atta. 19th. T.M.B.) M.C. No. 6078 L/Sgt. A. Morton Military Medal No. L/Cpl. A.H. Munn Military Medal	
	January 14th.		A message came from the Army Corps Commander stating that No. 7430 Rfn. Sievewright had been awarded the Military Medal for devotion to duty under the following circumstances. "On the night of 30/31st October, 1916, near LABOURFS Fm. Sievewright was told off to guide up a relief of the 2nd. Worcestershire regiment to the front line. The party passed through a barrage which caused casualties to all the officers of the company. Rfn. Sievewright, though himself wounded, took charge of the party and guided them up to the front line. He then waited	

Army Form C. 2118.

WAR DIARY
or
INTELLIGENCE SUMMARY

(Erase heading not required.)

Instructions regarding War Diaries and Intelligence Summaries are contained in F.S. Regs., Part II. and the Staff Manual respectively. Title Pages will be prepared in manuscript.

Place	Date	Hour	Summary of Events and Information	Remarks and references to Appendices
	January 14th.(contd.)		and guided down the relieved company."	
	January 17th.		The Battalion entrained at PONT REMY station at about 10.30 a.m. and detrained at BRAY-TOURLANDS at about 7 p.m. from where it marched to Camp 111, a distance of about 5 miles.	
	January 19th.		The Battalion marched to SUZANNE where it was accomodated in tents.	
	January 20th.		The Battalion moved into trenches in front of CLERY taking over from the 2nd. Battalion of the 90th. Infantry Regiment of the French. The relief went off very smoothly the French doing their utmost to make things easy, though all conversation was carried on in French. The hard frost made the marching easy, and also made the transport of ammunition, bombs tools, stores etc. practicable. The French was on the crest of a hill The line taken over from MONT ST. QUENTIN, and the sector held by the Battalion was over 1,000 yards North of the Somme.	
	January 25th.		The Battalion was relieved by the 2nd. Battalion Royal Welsh Fusiliers and took over their position in support trenches North of CLERY. There were numerous and good dugouts the French having put a great deal of work on accomodation of this kind. Their communication trenches were of extraordinary length.	
	January 28th.		The Battalion moved back to its former position relieving the 2nd. Royal Welsh Fusiliers. The weather was still hard and frosty which was very fortunate enabling the mules to bring up ammunition and stores. The only work that could be done was wiring as no impression could be made on the ground by digging. Large quantities of stores were brought up ready for use when the frost would break. at the outset of the tour of trenches considerable annoyance was caused by small enemy aerial torpedoes and also minnenwerfers. This was kept down by prompt artillery action and stores	

2449 Wt. W14957/M90 750,000 1/16 J.B.C. & A. Forms/C.2118/12.

Army Form C. 2118.

WAR DIARY
or
INTELLIGENCE=SUMMARY

(Erase heading not required.)

Instructions regarding War Diaries and Intelligence Summaries are contained in F. S. Regs., Part II. and the Staff Manual respectively. Title Pages will be prepared in manuscript.

Place	Date	Hour	Summary of Events and Information	Remarks and references to Appendices
	January 27th.		The German Emperor's birthday passed off quite quietly despite the fact that the wind favoured gas.	
	January 29th.		The battalion was relieved by the 2nd. Royal Welsh Fusiliers and took over former position north of CLERY.	
	January 31st.		The battalion was relieved by the 4th. Suffolks and proceeded to Camp 19, near SUZANNE.	
			Casualties during the month:-	
			Wounded: 9 other ranks.	
			Reinforcements:- Captain A.M.Alexander.	
			" K.A.Brown.	
			" D.S.Arthur.	
			Lieut. W.P.Sproul.	
			" W.C.Paterson.	
			2/Lieut.A.D.Cameron.	
			Major J.H.Keith (attached)	
			202 other ranks.	
			Strength at date:- 46 Officers: 1073 other ranks.	
			ERClark Lt. Col.,	
			Commanding 5th. Scottish Rifles.	

Army Form C. 2118.

WAR DIARY
or
INTELLIGENCE SUMMARY.
(Erase heading not required.)

Vol 28

19/33

5th. Scottish Rifles. Summary of Events and Information. February 1917.

Place	Date	Hour	Summary of Events and Information	Remarks and references to Appendices
	1st.- 3rd. February.		The Battn. remained at Camp 19. near SUZANNE.	
	4th. February.		The Battn. moved to FRISE BEND acting as Bde. reserve for 99th. Bde. One company was stationed at HOWITZER WOOD and a detachment of 2 platoons at CANLECOURT. The weather was very cold all the time with hard frost. The SOMME was frozen over.	
	8th. February.		The Bde. moved into the line again, and the Battn. moved to HOWITZER WOOD in Bde reserve. A great deal of carrying had to be done from here, in anticipation of an attack planned for the 2nd. R.W.F. and 20th. R.F.	
	12th. February.		The Battn. moved into the left subsection of the BETHUNE ROAD SECTOR relieving the 2nd. R.W.F. This sector was just south of BOUCHAVESNES Two companies were in the line and two in support. The enemy displayed some activity with minenwerfers, field guns and howitzers; but no great damage resulted.	
	15th. February.		About 8 am. under cover of an minenwerfer bombardment the Boschos blew a small mine in the centre of the BETHUNE ROAD, connecting up a sap of their's, about 50 yards from our lines. Arrangements were promptly made to deal with them. The distance was ranged by rifle grenades and stokes mortars. When every thing was ready the rifle grenades and stokes mortars fired into the crater for a ½ of an hour. At the same time the field guns put a barrage on the enemy trench mortars emplacements. The latter made no reply. 2nd	
	16th. February.		The Battn. was relieved by the ~~17th~~. R.W.F. and proceeded to ROAD WOOD. Shortly before the relief took place the enemy minenwerfered the Battn. Hdqrs., causing some casualties. Regt. Sgt. Major Woodbridge and 3 others being killed. The Battn. remained in ROAD WOOD and continued to supply carrying parties. Owing to the frost breaking and subsequent muddy state of the ground, the attack was postponed.	

Army Form C. 2118.

WAR DIARY
or
INTELLIGENCE SUMMARY.

(Erase heading not required.)

5th. Scottish Rifles.   Summary of Events and Information   February 1917.

Place	Date	Hour	Summary of Events and Information	Remarks and references to Appendices
	20th. February.		The Battn. relieved the 20th. N.F. in the right subsection with 3 coys. in the line and one in support. The trenches were in an appalling state mostly knee deep in mud and water. The dugouts were flooded and great difficulty was experienced in getting hot food. On account of these conditions, the attack was cancelled. The part the Battn. was to taken in it, was taking over from the 2nd. K.W.F. and 20th. N.F. the night after the assault.	
	24th. February.		The Battn. was relieved by the 2nd. A.& S.H., 93th. Bde. and moved to LOWITZER WOOD.	
	25th. February.		The Battn. was relieved by the 4th. Suffolk's and moved back again to Camp 19. SUZANNE.	
			REINFORCEMENTS RECEIVED.	

			Officers. Lieut. R.W.Begg.
			                    Lieut. R.W.McEwan.
			                    2/Lt. G.Gunn.
			                    2/Lt. A.S.Hamilton.
			                    2/Lt. J.Meikle.
			
			    Other Ranks. 61.
			
			    Casualties.
			
			    Officers. 2/Lt. J.C.Stuart. Wounded. 10/2/17.
			    Warrant Officers. 10140 R.S.M. J.H.Woodbridge. Killed.
			    Other Ranks. Killed. 22
			                    Wounded. 12
			                    Missing. 3	

Army Form C. 2118.

WAR DIARY
or
INTELLIGENCE SUMMARY.
(Erase heading not required.)

5th. Scottish Rifles. Summary of Events and Information. February 1917.

Place	Date	Hour	Summary of Events and Information	Remarks and references to Appendices
			Battalion Strength.	
			Officers. 49	
			Other Ranks. 938	
			Aly W Sprus Major,	
			Commanding 5th. Scottish Rifles.	

Instructions regarding War Diaries and Intelligence Summaries are contained in F. S. Regs., Part II. and the Staff Manual respectively. Title pages will be prepared in manuscript.

Army Form C. 2118.

WAR DIARY
or
INTELLIGENCE-SUMMARY.

(Erase heading not required.)

March 1917.

1st Scottish Rifles.

Vol 29

Place	Date	Hour	Summary of Events and Information	Remarks and references to Appendices
5th. Scottish Rifles.	1st. - 4th.		The battn. remained at Camp 19, near SUZANNE.	
	5th.		The battn. relieved the 9th. H.L.I. at FRISE BEND, with one Coy. at HOWITZER WOOD and two platoons at CAMBCOURT.	
	6th.		The Coy. at HOWITZER WOOD moved up to the 2nd. line on the MONACO-CURLY ROAD, being attached to the 1st. Battn. The Cameronians.	
	7th.		The battn. was relieved in all the above places by the 12th. South Wales Borderers of the 40th. Division, and moved into tents at SUZANNE. This was very uncomfortable as there was a very cold wind and hard frost.	
	8th.		The battn. moved back to Camp 13 north of CAPPLAY. The 2nd. A.W.F. & 1st. Battn. the Cameronians were in the same camp.	
	9th. - 31st.		The battn. remained at Camp 13, doing intensive training. Particular attention was paid to the training of platoons for open warfare, especially in the attack. Conferences for officers and also for each platoon were held, the former consisting both of lectures and working out schemes on the ground. At the latter the daily Intelligence Summaries and news in the papers was gone over and various points of the advance were explained. Instruction was also given to N.C.Os. and scouts in map reading and the use of ground. Inter-section shooting competitions at bottles and Lewis gun competitions were organised which were found to stimulate the interest of the men considerably. During the whole time the weather was changeable, but on the whole fine.	

Army Form C. 2118.

WAR DIARY
or
INTELLIGENCE SUMMARY.
(Erase heading not required.)

Place	Date	Hour	Summary of Events and Information	Remarks and references to Appendices
5th. Scottish Rifles.			March 1917.	
			Reinforcements arrived during the month.	
			Officers. Lieut. J.M.Blair.	
			2/Lt. R.A.Wood.	
			2/Lt. G.Moir.	
			2/Lt. C.J.Cheyne.	
			Other Ranks. 72.	
			Strength of Battalion.	
			Officers. 50.	
			Other Ranks. 1029.	
			E.R.Clough Lt. Col.,	
			Commanding 5th. Scottish Rifles.	
			30th. March 1917.	

Instructions regarding War Diaries and Intelligence Summaries are contained in F. S. Regs., Part II. and the Staff Manual respectively. Title pages will be prepared in manuscript.

Ref. map. Sheet 51B. S.W.
1:20.000

Instructions regarding War Diaries and Intelligence Summaries are contained in F. S. Regs., Part II. and the Staff Manual respectively. Title pages will be prepared in manuscript.

WAR DIARY
INTELLIGENCE-SUMMARY.
(Erase heading not required.)

Army Form C. 2118.

Seven appendices attached

5 dos Nat.

Place	Date	Hour	Summary of Events and Information	Remarks and references to Appendices
5th. Scottish Rifles.			APRIL 1917	
	1st.		The Battalion prepared to move from Camp 13 north of CHIPILLY.	
	2nd.		The Battn. marched to CORBIE where it was billeted for the night.	
	3rd.		The Battn. moved to COISY, a small village about 5 miles NORTH of AMIENS.	
DOULLENS.	4th.		The Battn. moved to BEAUVAL a town about 3 miles SOUTH of DOULLENS.	
	5th.		The Battn. marched to LUCHEUX passing through DOULLENS on the way.	
	7th.		After resting the previous day the Battn. marched to ST. AMAND and was quartered in the huts there. The quarters were the same as had been occupied in September last year.	
	8th.		The Battn. marched to BAILLEULMONT, a small village about 8 miles SOUTH- WEST OF ARRAS where it occupied billets for three nights.	
	11th.		The Battn. moved off at about 5 p.m. and marched to the "SCHLANGEN REDOUBT" near MERCATEL. This consisted of several trenches behind the former German lines. The old trenches were crossed between BRETENCOURT and BLAIRVILLE. On the German side of the lines all the villages and trees had been levelled making the country more difficult to recognise. During the march snow fell heavily and as the trenches afforded little shelter the troops were fairly uncomfortable.	
	12th.		The Battn. marched to near HENIN- SUR - COJEUL, bivouacing about the sunken roads and old trenches on the north side of the village. The enemy shelled the vicinity of the village, but the Battn. had few casualties with the exception of the Transport Officer, Lieut. A.E. STRUTHERS, the Quartermaster Hon. Lieut. J.BROWN and the Regimental	

WAR DIARY continued.
or
INTELLIGENCE SUMMARY.
(Erase heading not required.)

Army Form C. 2118.

Place	Date	Hour	Summary of Events and Information April 1917	Remarks and references to Appendices
5th. Scottish Rifles.	13th.		Sergeant Major (A.F.) TODD of the 1st. Battn. The Cameronians) all of whom were wounded by one shell which landed beside the Battn. Hqrs.	
			The Battn. remained in its bivouacs, warning was given of an approaching attack the following day to be carried out by the 1st. Battn. The Cameronians and the 20th. Royal Fusiliers with the 5th. Scottish Rifles in support. The ground the Battn. was likely to occupy was therefore reconnoitered by some of the officers of the Battn. About 10.30 p.m. orders for the following day were received the Battn. being detailed to attack on the left in place of the 20/R.F. who were in support.	See appendix Nos. 1 & 2
	14th.		The Battn. having had breakfast moved from HENIN-SUR-COJEUL at 2.30 a.m. and marched past ST. MARTIN-SUR-COJEUL through the HINDENBURGH LINE and deployed into lines of sections facing approximately EAST on the high ground due EAST of ST. MARTIN-S-COJEUL on the WESTERN side of the crest. (About N.34.d. and N.35.c. Ref. map sheet 51b. S.W. 1/20,000)	See appendix No.3
			The 56th. Division could be seen as the light grew stronger on the left. There was no liaison with the Cameronians.	
			At 5.30 a.m. as soon as the artillery opened fire, the leading line (C.Coy. under Captain L.R.R.Mailoch on the right; D. Coy. under Capt. K.Asenby brown on the left) advanced over the crest. (N.35.a & c) immediately coming under artillery and machine gun fire. The companies moved in artillery formation and extended as soon as compelled to do so by the enemy's fire.	
			The enemy put up a weak barrage in rear of the two leading coys. The rear slopes of the hill in N.34.c & c. were swept by machine gun fire.	
			Considerable difficulty was experienced in finding a position for Battn. Hdqrs. from whence the progress of the firing line could be seen. The difficulty was increased as the attack was made towards the East and consequently against the light. Visibility was therefore very low. The Battn. Hdqrs. was eventually established in the HINDENBURGH SUPPORT LINE	

WAR DIARY (Continued) or INTELLIGENCE-SUMMARY.

(Erase heading not required.)

Army Form C. 2118.

Place	Date	Hour	Summary of Events and Information	Remarks and references to Appendices
5th. Scottish Rifles.	14th.		April 1917	

The enemy's machine gun fire continued. At 6.30 a.m. a message was received, sent off at 6.5 a.m. that "C" Coy. was held up by machine gun fire, but hoped to push on.

At 7.35 a.m. it was possible to see the leading companies digging in below the crest of the first Objective. Nothing could be seen of the left and the position of the 56th. Division remained uncertain. A message was received at 8.10 a.m. (sent off at 6.50 a.m.) from O.C. "C" Coy. stating that he had reached a line about N.35.d.6.5. - N.35.d. 6.7. and was digging in. The runner who delivered this message stated that Capt. Brown O.C. Left Coy. had been killed.

The remains of the first two lines organised a position and hold on to it for the remainder of the day.

About 9 a.m. a message was received from the Brigade Hdqrs that endeavours were to be made to work round the left flank of the position already held. Up to this time no information had come in as to the position of the 56th. Division which should have been on the left of the Battn. and which should presumably have been ready to carry out such an operation. After some difficulty an officer of the Right Battn. of the 56th. Division (Queen Victoria's Rifles) was found in his own line, but no information of the position could be obtained. Indications pointed to no progress having been made. No assistance was therefore to be expected from the Left.

Arrangements were made with a Battery Commander for a Bombardment of the enemy's position to begin at 12 noon. The Batteries available were 4, 18 pounders and 1, 4.5 Howitzer. Orders were given to O.C. "B" Coy. (2/Lt. A. Downie) to advance at 12 noon with 2 Platoons on the left of the position already held and to attempt to work forward. This operation failed, 2/Lt. Downie being wounded, and a certain number of casualties being sustained.

At 12.30 p.m. the artillery fire was stopped.

Beyond covering the advanced line with artillery fire, when hostile machine gun fire was directed on them, no more could be done.

The Battn. was relieved by the 20/ Royal Fusiliers at night and occupied support trenches.

Army Form C. 2118.

WAR DIARY (continued) or INTELLIGENCE SUMMARY.

(Erase heading not required.)

Instructions regarding War Diaries and Intelligence Summaries are contained in F. S. Regs., Part II. and the Staff Manual respectively. Title pages will be prepared in manuscript.

Place	Date	Hour	Summary of Events and Information	Remarks and references to Appendices
5th. Scottish Rifles.			April 1917.	
	14th.		During the day the Battn. had made an advance of over 800 yards, had dug in and held the ground won. The casualties for the day were :—	
			3 Officers Killed.	
			59 Other Ranks Killed.	
			5 Officers Wounded.	
			155 Other Ranks Wounded.	
			14 Other Ranks Missing.	
			The officers were :—	
			Captain. K. ASHBY BROWN. Killed.	
			Lieut. A.W.McEWAN. "	
			2/Lt. D.MURCHISON. "	
			J.T.WILLIE. Wounded.	
			A.G.McCULLOCH. "	
			D.WOOD. "	
			A.M.YOUNG. "	
			R.DOWNIE. "	
	15th.		The Battn. remained in the trenches taken over from the 20/R.F. and was relieved late at night by the 1st. Middlesex Regt. and 2/ Argyll & Sutherland Highlanders. The Battn. proceeded to bivouacs south of HENIN-SUR-COJEUL and remained there for two days.	
	19th.		The Battn. relieved the 9/H.L.I. (The Glasgow Highlanders) in the sector on the right. This was held as an outpost line, the Coys. being dug in in sunken roads WEST OF CROISILLES & the SENSEE RIVER with posts out in front. The enemy (in the HINDENBURGH LINE) were over 1,000 yards away. The Battn. suffered no casualties.	
	21st.		The Battn. was again relieved by the 9/H.L.I. and moved to bivouacs at BOYELLES.	

Army Form C. 2118.

WAR DIARY (continued)
or
INTELLIGENCE SUMMARY.
(Erase heading not required.)

Place	Date	Hour	Summary of Events and Information	Remarks and references to Appendices
5th. Scottish Rifles.			April 1917	
	22nd.		The Battn. moved to north of HENIN-SUR-COJEUL relieving the 1st. Battn. Middlesex Regt.	
			Orders were received for an attack to be made by the Division the following day, the Battn. being part of the Divisional Reserve.	see No.4
	23rd.		At about 9 a.m. orders were received to move up and report at the Hdqrs. 98th. Bde.	see No.5
			On the way to the HINDENBURGH LINE bombs, rifle grenades and trench mortar bombs were picked up and carried up. The Battn. then filed into the tunnel which runs underneath the HINDENBURGH SUPPORT LINE and awaited further orders. The situation appeared to be that the 4th. Battn. Suffolk Regt. had bombed up a front and support lines of the HINDENBURGH LINE for about 1,000 yards, had taken about 700 prisoners and were then driven back to their original position, with the exception of 2 companies in the front line who appeared to be surrounded.	
			The 2/A.&.S.H. had made some progress but the 1st. Middlesex Regt. had been held up.	
		11.30 a.m.	At about 11.30 a.m. "C" Coy. 5/Scottish Rifles (under Capt. L.R.A.Malloch) was sent up under the orders of the C.O. of the 4th. Suffolk Regt. to the HINDENBURGH FRONT LINE. This Coy. advanced beyond the original block then came in touch with the enemy. With the help of some R.E. a new block was built.	
		1.30 p.m.	About 1.30 p.m. "B" Coy. (under 2/Lt. N.Clark) was ordered up to support "C" Coy. who had repelled a certain amount of bombing on the part of the enemy.	
		4.15 p.m.	About 4.15 p.m. orders were received from the 98th. Bde. verbally, afterwards in writing to make a bombing attack down the trench at 6.24 p.m. As one Coy. was employed policing the tunnel and two were under the orders of the 4th. Suffolk Regt. only 1 Coy. was available. All available men of the 4th. Battn. Kings (Liverpool Regt.) and the remnants of the 4th. Suffolk Regt. were placed under the orders of Lt. Col. E.K.Clayton D.S.O.. After a hasty reconnaissance of the block and survey of the resources in the way of bombs, rifle grenades	see No.6

Army Form C. 2118.

WAR DIARY
or
INTELLIGENCE SUMMARY.
(Erase heading not required.)

Place	Date	Hour	Summary of Events and Information April 1917	Remarks and references to Appendices
5th. Scottish Rifles.	23rd.		etc., "D" Coy. (under 2/Lt. D.A.RIGBY) was formed up ready for the attack. Covering fire of the Lewis guns and rifle grenades was arranged for with a Coy. of the 2nd. R.W.F. and an officer of the 11th. Field Coy. R.E. was detailed to be ready to construct a block. At 6.24 p.m. after a discharge of rifle grenades, bombing squads of "D" Coy. rushed over the block and round a few traverses. They encountered a heavy discharge of bombs and were held up by wire. They were driven back. The block was still held however. At 6.35 p.m. a message was received stating that the 2/Royal Welsh Fusiliers had been unable to get forward. "D" Coy. was then ordered to remain where it was. About 8 p.m. the enemy put on a heavy barrage of artillery rifle grenades and bombs. Whether they actually attacked or not is not definite, but considerable confusion resulted, rumours came back stating that they had rushed the block. 2/Lt. RIGBY was seriously wounded at the opening of the barrage and most of the N.C.Os. were killed or wounded, in consequence of which some of the men fell back. The Block was held by a small party of the 2/R.W.F. and 2 men of the 5th. Sco. Rifles. The shelling died down about 10.30 p.m. and nothing further was attempted by either side. "C" and "D" Coys. in the meantime had suffered fairly severe casualties by the enemy's shelling. At about 5.30 p.m. the two Coys. of the 4th. Suffolk Regt. which had been surrounded by the enemy managed to get back to the main trench.	
	24th.		The Battn. was relieved by Coys. of the 1st. Battn. The Cameronians about 7 a.m. The Coys. moved back to support trenches. About 8.30 a.m. information was received that the enemy had evacuated his position. This was confirmed. The 1st. Battn. the Cameronians pushed up the HINDENBURGH LINE meeting no opposition and the 20/Royal Fusiliers, pushed patrols over the crest of the hill which had been the first objective on the 14th. April.	

Army Form C. 2118.

WAR DIARY continued.
or
INTELLIGENCE SUMMARY.
(Erase heading not required.)

Place	Date	Hour	Summary of Events and Information	Remarks and references to Appendices
5th. Scottish Rifles.			April 1917	
	25th.		The Battn. was relieved by the 15th. Durham Light Infantry of the 21st. Division and moved back to BOYELLES.	
	26th.		The Division was relieved by the 21st. Division. The Battn. moved back to BLAIRVILLE where it occupied cellars and German dugouts.	
	27th.		The Battn. marched to BAILLEULMONT where it occupied its former billets. On the way the G.O.C. of VII Army Corps SIR T.D'O.SNOW watched the Battn. passing.	
	28th.-30th.		The Battn. remained at BAILLEULMONT and training was carried out on the usual lines.	

Casualties during the month.

Officers.		Other Ranks.	
Capt. K.A.Brown.	Killed in Action.	Killed in Action.	48
Lieut. R.W.McEwan.	do.	Wounded.	209
2/Lt. D.Murchison.	do.	Missing.	13
Lieut. A.F.Struthers.	Wounded.		
Hon. Lieut. J.Brown.	do.		
2/Lt. J.T.Wyllie.	do.		
2/Lt. D.Wood.	do.		
2/Lt. R.Downie.	do.		
2/Lt. R.M.Young.	do.		
2/Lt. C.G.Cheyne.	do.		
2/Lt. R.S.Hamilton.	do.		
2/Lt. M.G.McCulloch.	do.		
2/Lt. D.A.Rigby.	do.		

Reinforcement arrived during the month.

Officers.   Other Ranks.
Nil.   92

E.R.Clayton Lt. Col.,
Commanding 5th. Scottish Rifles.

WAR DIARY
or
INTELLIGENCE SUMMARY.

(Erase heading not required.)

Army Form C. 2118.

5 Sco. Rif.
19/33
Vol 31

Place	Date	Hour	Summary of Events and Information	Remarks and references to Appendices
			May 1917	
5/Scottish Rifles	1st May		The Battalion remained at BAILLEULMONT.	
	2nd May		The Battn. moved to MONCHY-AU-BOIS. As the village was immediately behind the old German lines, no houses or cellars were available. The weather was very hot. The Battn. bivouacks. The Battn. remained in MONCHY till the 11th May training being carried on in the usual lines.	
			On May 7th a Divisional race meeting was held.	
	12th May		The Division moved back into the line. The Battn. left MONCHY at 6.30 a.m. and marched to BOISLEUX-ST-MARC taking over a camp from the 9th H.L.I. The Brigade was in Divisional reserve.	
	15th May		The Battn. moved to ST. LEGER in reserve to	

Army Form C. 2118.

WAR DIARY
or
INTELLIGENCE SUMMARY.
(Erase heading not required.)

Instructions regarding War Diaries and Intelligence Summaries are contained in F. S. Regs., Part II. and the Staff Manual respectively. Title pages will be prepared in manuscript.

Place	Date	Hour	Summary of Events and Information	Remarks and references to Appendices
			the Brigade. A warning order was received that the Batt. would be required to carry out an attack on the 17th on the HINDENBURG LINE. Before issuing information was received that Batteries L.R.W. Willcock had been accorded the Military Cross. As part of the line where the Barbican was to attack was reconnoitred, but owing to the careful layering of the enemy trenches, any little information could be obtained. A particularly useful reconnaissance was carried out by No 242069 Sgt R. Lawson on the night of 15/16th. A full size model of "The trench" to part allotted to the Battalion was laid out in the fields and the attacking Companies practised in it. See the following two Maisons of the Casernieres	

WAR DIARY
or
INTELLIGENCE SUMMARY

Army Form C. 2118.

Instructions regarding War Diaries and Intelligence Summaries are contained in F. S. Regs., Part II. and the Staff Manual respectively. Title pages will be prepared in manuscript.

(Erase heading not required.)

Place	Date	Hour	Summary of Events and Information	Remarks and references to Appendices
	17th to 19th May		advanced towards the HINDENBURG LINE. They were fired on and suffered some casualties. They regained their former position after dark. There was then no doubt that the HINDENBURG LINE was held by the enemy. The attack was postponed until 20th May. The Battn. remained at ST. LEGER. Reconnaissances of the ground and wire were carried out by officers and N.C.O's and photographs were practiced on the model.	
	20th May		The Battn. moved off from ST. LEGER at 2.5 a.m. and took up positions ready for supsequent SE of CROISELLES at 3.15 a.m. At 4.35 a.m. the Battn. began to move into the position of deployment. Three attacking Coys. (each of three platoons 2 platoons of which attacked, the third being used as a moppers up party) "B" on the left numbered 2/13 M. Clark	

Army Form C. 2118.

WAR DIARY
or
INTELLIGENCE SUMMARY.
(Erase heading not required.)

Instructions regarding War Diaries and Intelligence Summaries are contained in F. S. Regs., Part II. and the Staff Manual respectively. Title pages will be prepared in manuscript.

Place	Date	Hour	Summary of Events and Information	Remarks and references to Appendices
			As the attack under Capt C.W.A. Gurnard D'arks right under 2/2 W. Wickkley) moved forward in touch with the 2/Worcestershire Regt. on the left. An officer of the 19/Lucs Batty was forward with the attacking Coys to reconnoitre positions for his guns. C. Coy under Capt T.W. Wallock MC. section of the M/Lucs Coys R.E. and 2 guns of the 19/Lucs Batty reviewed in a Quarry at M.19.a.2.2 Bde S.a. Batt. Headquarters. At 5.20 a.m. the fog which had thickened added to the trench of the burning shells was a cup. thick and the ground was the enemy's leave in very rough set up hy sheet line and the enemy's knee line obtained. It was then very difficult for boys to keep direction and for the man to recognise objects which which they were familiar on the march. About 5.17 a.m. scattered rifle shots were heard, by	

WAR DIARY
or
INTELLIGENCE SUMMARY

(Erase heading not required.)

Army Form C. 2118.

Place	Date	Hour	Summary of Events and Information	Remarks and references to Appendices
			3.15 a.m. this had grown to a considerable rifle and machine gun fire. A minute or two before the Field Artillery barrage came down on the enemies support line, sounds of cheering could be heard from the direction of the 100" Bde. B Coy advanced through the were without much difficulty and by C.an. the greater part of two platoons had reached a point about U.14.c.35.95. After this no sign since seen to have been near the enemy's support line. "A" Coy advanced as ordered to the enemy's front line soon after zero. "D" Coy appears to have met with much opposition than the nineties. A few were seen to have reached the enemy's front line, but the greater part were held up about the enemy's wire where they finally dug in. The result of the failure of the right (D) Coy was that the enemy could boom up his front from the	

WAR DIARY
or
INTELLIGENCE SUMMARY.
(Erase heading not required.)

Army Form C. 2118.

Place	Date	Hour	Summary of Events and Information	Remarks and references to Appendices

with cart and take in place the wire and less bays. This covered all cases been between 6:15 am and 7am. A temporary block which was put in by the enemy cop. was forced over the party of the enemy cop. which had gained the enemy's front line was pushed towards in was at O.M.P.2.9.

At 6.15 am the section of the 1/1 Field Coy. R.E. with carrying party entered the sap up to make the pre-arranged blocks in the front line. At 7am. Lance Corporal reports having been directed of the General situation; the section of the 191 Tun. Coy. which was on the enemy's cap engaged the endeavour that this section should take up a position covering the blocks, but owing to the paucity of ammunition, here was unable to be effective. At 7am an blocks from a Rifle attack. At 7am a carrying party of 1 officer and 20 other ranks of the 201. R.E. was accepted with bombs. At 7am owing to the uncertainty of the

WAR DIARY or INTELLIGENCE SUMMARY

Army Form C. 2118.

Place	Date	Hour	Summary of Events and Information	Remarks and references to Appendices

situation it was arranged that the right flank barrage by our artillery brigade of the Fifth Army should be continued after 7.15 a.m.

The first information obtained has indicated that all objectives had been taken. About 9 a.m. it became evident that the situation was not so favourable and was reported. Reports were sent that the firing line of heavy and field artillery should be continued.

At 10 a.m. in response to an urgent request for bombs a carrying party of 1 officer and 27 other ranks was sent off. Both of the carrying parties suffered considerable casualties, the officers being wounded in each case.

The situation of the companies remained as previously described and were not affected by the attack of the Canadians and were 20/ R.F. on the left of the 100 Bde. at 7.30 a.m. but at about 10 p.m. the advanced party of the

WAR DIARY or INTELLIGENCE SUMMARY

Army Form C. 2118.

(Erase heading not required.)

Place	Date	Hour	Summary of Events and Information	Remarks and references to Appendices
			left coy; together with the right coy of the 2/10 Worcestershire Regt. appear to have come back in the enemy's original front line.	
			Owing to its isolated position no carrying parties were able to reach the right (D) Coy on the night 20/21st. The reserve (C) Coy relieved part of A & B Coys during the night. Some difficulty was experienced in joining up with the latter on the right, this was overcome on the 21st and food came had not been brought in touch with D Coy.	
	22nd Aug.		The Batten was relieved by the 4/ Northumberland Fusiliers and moved back to ST. LEGER. The work of reorganization was taken up at once, owing to casualties the Batte. was organised into two Coys. The casualties among officers for the relieve were:— Captain C.W.A. Green — Killed	

WAR DIARY
or
INTELLIGENCE SUMMARY.
(Erase heading not required.)

Army Form C. 2118.

Place	Date	Hour	Summary of Events and Information	Remarks and references to Appendices
			2/Lt. H.CLARK wounded	
			" J.MEIKLE "	
			" J.I.SCOTT "	
			" J.OWEN. "	
			" A.S.COLLINS "	
			" J.M.MAGUIRE "	
			Casualties for other ranks 145.	
			The Battn received at ST.LEGER the work of relieving being carried out.	
	26ᵗʰ May/-		Orders were issued for a further attack on the HINDENBURG LINE by the 19/Inf Bde to be carried out by the 2/R.W.F. and the Cameronians. A carrying party of 100 men from the 5/ Sco. Rif were attached to each of these from the night of the 26ᵗʰ.	
	27ᵗʰ May/-		At 1.50 pm the 2/ R.W.F. and the Cameronians attacked the HINDENBURG Support Line in three waves	

WAR DIARY
INTELLIGENCE SUMMARY
(Erase heading not required.)

Army Form C. 2118.

Place	Date	Hour	Summary of Events and Information	Remarks and references to Appendices
	28th cont.		The 5/Lco. Rif. carrying parties went over in rear of the third wave. The attack was unsuccessful, the trench was reached, but could not be consolidated and the troops fell back to their original line. The 5/Lco. Rif. suffered 42 casualties. The two coys. attached to the 2/R.W.F. and the Cameronians were relieved and rejoined the remainder of the Battn. West of ST. LEGER.	
	31st May		The Battn. moved to BELLACOURT. Casualties during the month. Officers. Capt. & Adj. Lucien Heller on action 20/5/17 2/Lt. A.S. Bolden wounded " " " " M. Clark " " " " J. Meeke " " " " Gwilaguine " " " " J. Owen " "	

WAR DIARY
INTELLIGENCE SUMMARY
(Erase heading not required.)

Army Form C. 2118.

Place	Date	Hour	Summary of Events and Information	Remarks and references to Appendices
			2/Lt. S.S. Scott wounded 21/5/17	
			Other ranks	
			Killed in action 25	
			wounded 97	
			missing 33	
			wounded & missing 13	
			missing believed killed 2	
			wounded at duty 16	
			186	
			Reinforcements received during the month	
			Officers Lt. W.G.A. Turner, 2/Lt. A. Thom	
			2/Lt. J.R. Grant, " R. Leplar	
			" J.M. Wood " D.A. Buchanan	
			" R. Davie " J. Bardu	
			" S. Craig " D. Chapman	
			Other ranks. 57	

Army Form C. 2118.

WAR DIARY
or
INTELLIGENCE SUMMARY.
(Erase heading not required.)

Place	Date	Hour	Summary of Events and Information	Remarks and references to Appendices
			Battalion Strength. Officers 35 Other ranks. 633 E R Clayton Lt Col. Commanding 5/Scottish Rifles	

Instructions regarding War Diaries and Intelligence Summaries are contained in F. S. Regs., Part II. and the Staff Manual respectively. Title pages will be prepared in manuscript.

Army Form C. 2118.

WAR DIARY
or
INTELLIGENCE SUMMARY.
(Erase heading not required.)

Vol 32

5th SCOTTISH RIFLES.   Summary of Events and Information   JUNE, 1917.

Place	Date	Hour	Summary of Events and Information	Remarks and references to Appendices
	JUNE 1st - 16th.		The Battalion remained at BULLECOURT. Companies were reorganised into three platoons each and training was carried out. Special attention was paid to musketry. Ranges were put in order in the old "No Man's Land". The Battalion was also put through a Field Firing Exercise. The usual training of specialists was carried out.	
			On 4th June the Battalion was inspected by the Army Corps Commander. Whilst out of the line 8 new officers joined but the men were not made up to strength.	
	JUNE 17th.		At a Brigade Church Parade of all denominations Lieut.General Sir T. D'O.Snow,K.C.B.,K.C.M.G., commanding the VIIth Army Corps, addressed the Brigade and presented medal ribbons of decorations won in the recent fighting to the following:-	
			240032 Captain L.K.M.Malloch, "A" Coy. Military Cross.	
			200629 Sgt. A.Peat., "C" " Military Medal.	
			200251 L/ " P.Docherty, "A" " " "	
			" T.F.Wilkinson, " "	

Army Form C. 2118.

WAR DIARY
INTELLIGENCE SUMMARY.
(Erase heading not required.)

Instructions regarding War Diaries and Intelligence Summaries are contained in F. S. Regs., Part II. and the Staff Manual respectively. Title pages will be prepared in manuscript.

Place	Date	Hour	Summary of Events and Information	Remarks and references to Appendices
			JUNE, 1917.	
			5th SCOTTISH RIFLES.	
			202245 L/Sgt. A.Raymond, "C"Coy., Military Medal.	
			240326 Cpl. R.Webb, "D" " "	
			202349 L/Cpl. R.Ritchie,",", "D" " "	
			200294 " J.T.McQuat, "D" " "	
			200290 Rfn. H.L.Thom,(Cyclist) "B" " "	
			200256 " F.R.R.Butters,(Cyclist)"B" " "	
			In the afternoon Battalion sports were held.(See Appendix 1.)	
	JUNE 18th.		The Division moved into the line relieving the 21st Division. The battalion proceeded to Camp B MOYENNEVILLE relieving the 1st Lincolnshire Regiment.	
	JUNE 19th.		The Brigade took over the right sector of the Divisional Front.The Battalion relieved the 7th Battalion Leicestershire Regiment.in Brigade Reserve.	
	JUNE 22nd.		The Battalion relieved the 2/R.W.F. in the front line. Nothing of note happened while the battalion held the line.A good deal of work was done in wiring,digging T heads out from the front line and revetting with sandbags	

Army Form C. 2118.

WAR DIARY
or
INTELLIGENCE SUMMARY.
(Erase heading not required.)

Summary of Events and Information

5th SCOTTISH RIFLES.

June, 1917.

Place	Date	Hour	Summary of Events and Information	Remarks and references to Appendices
MOYENNEVILLE.	JUNE 27th.		The Battalion was relieved by the 9th H.L.I. and moved back to Camp A.	
	JUNE 29th.		The Divisional was relieved by the 31st Division.	
			The Battalion marched from MOYENNEVILLE to MONCHY-AU-BOIS.	
			CASUALTIES DURING MONTH.	
			Killed 4 Other Ranks.	
			Wounded 8 " "	
			REINFORCEMENTS RECEIVED DURING MONTH.	
			Officers. Other Ranks.	
			2/Lt.J.C.Fletcher. 156	
			" A.R.MacGregor.	
			" W.McClintock.	
			" H.F.Patterson.	
			" W.Gavin.	

Army Form C. 2118.

WAR DIARY
or
INTELLIGENCE SUMMARY.
(Erase heading not required.)

Instructions regarding War Diaries and Intelligence Summaries are contained in F. S. Regs., Part II. and the Staff Manual respectively. Title pages will be prepared in manuscript.

Place	Date	Hour	Summary of Events and Information	Remarks and references to Appendices
5th SCOTTISH RIFLES.			JUNE, 1917.	
			Officers. Other Ranks.	
			2/Lt.A.H.Frame.	
			" R.Cameron.	
			" P.Binnie.	
			STRENGTH OF BATTALION.	
			Officers. Other Ranks.	
			40 792	

J.R.Clayton Lieut.Colonel,
Commanding 5th Scottish Rifles.

Army Form C. 2118.

5/6 Scottish Rifles
1 of 33

WAR DIARY
or
INTELLIGENCE SUMMARY.
(Erase heading not required.)

Instructions regarding War Diaries and Intelligence Summaries are contained in F. S. Regs., Part II. and the Staff Manual respectively. Title pages will be prepared in manuscript.

Place	Date	Hour	Summary of Events and Information	Remarks and references to Appendices
5th SCOTTISH RIFLES			July 1917.	
	1st		The Battalion remained at MONCHY-AU-BOIS.	
	2nd		The Brigade resumed the march back to the rest area. The Battalion marching to LEALVILLERS.	
	3rd		The Battalion marched to TALMAS.	
	4th		The Battalion marched to LA CHAUSSEE.	
	5th		The Brigade completed the move. The 5th.Scottish Rifles along with the 2nd.R.W.F. and the 2 Bn.R.F. were billeted in AIRAINES. The Cameronians at CONDE-FOLIE about 4 miles away. The Battalion remained at AIRAINES during the remainder of the month. Training was carried out daily except Sundays. A draft of 170 other ranks arrived on the 7th July. This brought the Battalion [illegible] up to strength. The training of bombers, Lewis Gunners and Signallers was carried out, as well as the general training in the attack, open and wood fighting. Several Battalion schemes were carried out. The Brigade route marched twice a week. On July 17th. and 18th. a Divisional Horse Show was	

Army Form C. 2118.

WAR DIARY
or
INTELLIGENCE SUMMARY.
(Erase heading not required.)

Instructions regarding War Diaries and Intelligence Summaries are contained in F. S. Regs., Part II. and the Staff Manual respectively. Title pages will be prepared in manuscript.

Place	Date	Hour	Summary of Events and Information	Remarks and references to Appendices
	3/-		was/ held near Cavillon, a few entries were put in by this Battalion, but no prizes were won. On July 20th. and 21st. a Divisional Scheme was carried out on ground from near CONDE FOLIE to north of PICQUIGNY. The Brigade prepared to entrain at Pont Remy for DUNKERQUE on the night of July 31st./August 1st.	
			REINFORCEMENTS RECEIVED DURING THE MONTH.	
			OFFICERS. OTHER RANKS.	
			Major C.C.Scott. 204.	
			STRENGTH OF BATTALION.	
			OFFICERS. OTHER RANKS.	
			40. 952.	

E.W.Clayfirst., Colonel,
Commanding 5th Scottish Rifles.—

Army Form C. 2118.

WAR DIARY
or
INTELLIGENCE SUMMARY.
(Erase heading not required.)

Instructions regarding War Diaries and Intelligence Summaries are contained in F. S. Regs., Part II. and the Staff Manual respectively. Title pages will be prepared in manuscript.

5TH SCOTTISH RIFLES.   AUGUST 1914.

Place	Date	Hour	Summary of Events and Information	Remarks and references to Appendices
	1st		The Battalion entrained at PONT REMY Station early in the morning and arrived at DUNKERQUE about 11p.m. It was then conveyed in barges to BRAY DUNES where it was billeted. The Brigade was camped among the Sand dunes beside the coast. Training was continued in the usual lines though the ground was somewhat limited. Bathing parades were held in the afternoons.	
	15th		The Battalion moved to COXYDE where the transport remained.	
	16th		The battalion relieved the 5th Sm.rwest Riding Regiment in support in the LOMBARTZIDE Sector. Dugouts and trenches in the REDAN, an old fortification of NIEUPORT, on the East bank of the Yser, being occupied.	
	21st		The Battalion relieved the 20th Royal Fusiliers in the right sub-sector. The condition of the Line was very bad, owing to the flat low lying ground. Breastworks were the only protection, these in the majority of posts were not bullet proof. There were a few dugouts strengthened with concrete. The breastworks were not continuous being only in a state of repair at the posts. The approach was over three fourteen bridges /	

A6945 Wt. W14422/M1160 350,000. 12/16 D. D. & L. Forms/C./2118/14.

Army Form C. 2118.

WAR DIARY
or
INTELLIGENCE SUMMARY.
(Erase heading not required.)

Instructions regarding War Diaries and Intelligence Summaries are contained in F. S. Regs, Part II. and the Staff Manual respectively. Title pages will be prepared in manuscript.

Place	Date	Hour	Summary of Events and Information	Remarks and references to Appendices
			On 18th. August, Lieut.,Colonel E.R.Clayton D.S.O. was appointed General Staff Officer, 2nd. Grade, of the VIth. Army Corps, and left the Battalion that day. Major H.B.Spens was appointed to Command, and Major C.C.Scott second in command.	
			The following farewell order by Lieut.,Colonel E.R.Clayton D.S.O. was published.	
			" In giving up the Command of the 5th Scottish Rifles I wish to express to all ranks my appreciation of the good work which has been done during the twelve months in which I have been in Command, and my best wishes for the future. The success of a Battalion depends on every Officer and every man doing his duty, whether employed as a Company or Platoon Commander, a Lewis Gunner, Transport Driver, Rifleman, Runner, or in any other capacity. It is this devotion to duty which has enabled the Battalion to do well in the past, and which will enable you to do still better in the future.	
			I wish you all the best of luck, and expect to hear of the 5th. Scottish Rifles doing great things in the future."	

A6945 Wt.W14422/M1160 350.000 12/16 D.D. &L. Forms/C/2118/14.

WAR DIARY
or
INTELLIGENCE SUMMARY.
(Erase heading not required.)

Army Form C. 2118.

Place	Date	Hour	Summary of Events and Information	Remarks and references to Appendices
			AUGUST.	
			the southern environs.	
			bridges, and a permanent bridge over five lock gates of the canals, all	
			these were subjected to systematic shelling and the portions were	
			frequently broken down.	
			Headquarters and Reserve Company in the Alpha was shelled heavily	
			shelled by 4.2 Howitzers and 5.9 as well as Heavies and	
			9th the area was shot upon by a considerable amount of	
			15 inch gun. Consequently the amount of Casualties amongst	
			was very slight, though the demoralisation amongst the inhabitants	
			The front line trenches escaped practically all shelling	
	27.		The Division was relieved by the 30th Division, the Battalion being	
			relieved by the 5/6th. Royal Scots. After the relief the Battalion	
			marched to the PLACE.	
	29.		The Battalion moved by Motor Busses to PONT DECHLIN, a suburb of DUNKERQUE	
			on the west side of the town.	
	31.		The Battalion moved by Motor Busses to HOULLE, a small village, 5 miles	
			North West of SAINT OMER.	

Army Form C. 2118.

WAR DIARY
or
INTELLIGENCE SUMMARY.
(Erase heading not required.)

REINFORCEMENT RECEIVED DURING THE MONTH.

	Officers.	Other Ranks,
Lieut. J.S.Hardie (5th. Sco. Rif.)		53.
" P.A. McWilliams, (Ayrshire Yeomanry.)		

CASUALTIES DURING THE MONTH.

	Other Ranks.
Killed in Action.	3.
Died of Wounds.	1.
Wounded.	47.
Wounded at Duty.	4.

STRENGTH OF BATTALION.

Officers.	42.
Other Ranks.	909.

[signature]
Major,
Commanding, 5th Scottish Rifles.—

Army Form C. 2118.

WAR DIARY
or
INTELLIGENCE SUMMARY.
(Erase heading not required.)

Summary of Events and Information

REINFORCEMENT RECEIVED DURING THE MONTH.

Officers.	Other Ranks.
Lieut., J.S. Mardie (6th. Scottish Rifles.)	53.
Lt. & Q.M. P.A. McWilliams, (Ayrshire Yeomanry.)	

CASUALTIES DURING THE MONTH.

	Other Ranks.
Killed in Action.	3.
Died of Wounds.	1.
Wounded.	47.
Wounded at Duty.	4.

STRENGTH OF BATTALION.

| Officers. | 42. |
| Other Ranks. | 909. |

[signature]
Major,
Commanding 5th Scottish Rifles.

Army Form C. 2118.

WAR DIARY
or
INTELLIGENCE SUMMARY.
(Erase heading not required.)

1/5 Scottish Rifles
19/33
Vol 35 (analysed 1/6)

36. O
19/11/16

Place	Date	Hour	Summary of Events and Information	Remarks and references to Appendices
			5TH SCOTTISH RIFLES.	
			SEPTEMBER, 1917.	
	1st - 14th.		The Battalion remained at HOULLE. Training was carried on.	
			The X Corps front EAST of YPRES near the YPRES - MENIN Road was reconnoitred by the Commanding Officer, Adjutant and Company Commanders.	
	15th.		The Battalion moved to LEDERZEELE.	
	16th.		The Battalion moved to STEENVOORDE via CASSEL.	
	17th.		The Battalion moved to GODEWAERSVELDE.	
	20th.		The Battalion moved to YORK Camp about 1 mile NORTH of WESTOUTRE.	
	24th.		The Battalion moved to BEDFORD HOUSE.	
	25th.		Early in the morning Lt.-Col. H.B.Spens was ordered to reconnoitre a position of close support to the 98th Infantry Brigade While accompanying him in so doing 2/Lt. A.S.Collins was killed by a shell. The Battalion moved up to this position in J 13 c & d at 1 p.m. (see Appendix 11.)	
			At about 3 p.m. orders were received from the 98th Infantry	

Army Form C. 2118.

WAR DIARY
or
INTELLIGENCE SUMMARY.
(Erase heading not required.)

Instructions regarding War Diaries and Intelligence Summaries are contained in F. S. Regs., Part II. and the Staff Manual respectively. Title pages will be prepared in manuscript.

Place	Date	Hour	Summary of Events and Information	Remarks and references to Appendices
	26th.		Brigade, to whom the battalion was attached to attack along with the 4th Battalion Suffolk Regiment at Zero 5.50 a.m. on 26th September, 1917. (See Appendix III.) The positions of the front lines of both the 98th Brigade and the enemy was uncertain. Guides were supplied but owing to the extremely difficult ground and lack of knowledge of the route by the guides, the Companies got lost. 2/Lt. P. Binnie was killed by a shell on the way up near the 98th Infantry Brigade Head-quarters. At 3.30 a.m. when none of our Companies had arrived, O.C. 4th Suffolks got permission from 98th Infantry brigade to move forward alone but did not do so then. Between that hour and 4.15 a.m. A & B Companies arrived and it was finally decided to move forward these Companies with the 4th Suffolks at 4.45 a.m. about 4.30 a.m. (Zero being at 5.50 a.m.) the enemy put down a heavy barrage. A & B Companies started to move at 4.45 a.m. but O.C. Suffolks decided to wait and the half battalion conformed. Finally at 5.25 a.m. A. & B Coys.	

A6945 Wt. W11422/M1190 350,000 12/16 D.D. & L. Forms/C/2118/14.

WAR DIARY
or
INTELLIGENCE SUMMARY.
(Erase heading not required.)

Army Form C. 2118.

Instructions regarding War Diaries and Intelligence Summaries are contained in F. S. Regs., Part II. and the Staff Manual respectively. Title pages will be prepared in manuscript.

Place	Date	Hour	Summary of Events and Information	Remarks and references to Appendices
			and the 4th Suffolks moved forward. Half C Company arrived shortly after -wards and moved forward in support.	
			Part of A & B Companies reached a line between BLACK WATCH CORNER and CARNISLA FARM and established themselves there. Owing to the heavy enemy barrage and a thick mist it was extremely difficult to keep direction and touch.	
		10.50 a.m.	D Company and most of the remainder of C Company arrived about They were ordered to advance at 11.15 a.m., sweep up all parties between battalion Head-quarters and the line at BLACK WATCH CORNER and carry the line on. The line was carried slightly forward and con- -solidated, a gap between the Australians and the 100th Brigade being thus filled up. Just about this time the Second Royal Welsh Fusiliers attacked across our front.	
			Early in the afternoon the position became very obscure and the brigade were anxious to get a reliable report. 2nd Lieut. D.W.MacLachlan acting adjutant, went forward through a heavy barrage and ascertained what	

A6945 Wt.W14422/M160 350,000 12/16 D.D. & L. Forms/C/2118/14.

WAR DIARY
or
INTELLIGENCE SUMMARY.
(Erase heading not required.)

Army Form C. 2118.

Instructions regarding War Diaries and Intelligence Summaries are contained in F. S. Regs., Part II. and the Staff Manual respectively. Title pages will be prepared in manuscript.

Place	Date	Hour	Summary of Events and Information	Remarks and references to Appendices
			the situation was. On his return he also had to pass through a barrage.	
			About 4.45 p.m. No 240101 Rfm W Hill D Company brought down an	
			enemy aeroplane by Lewis Gun fire. The aeroplane had been machine	
			gunning our position.	
			During the afternoon and night some counter attacks were beaten	
			off. The RED LINE was reported to be held by an AUSTRALIAN patrol but	
			as the result of a joint patrol with them this was found to be incorrect.	
			In consequence orders from the 98th Brigade for the Battalion to advance	
			to the BLUE LINE in the morning were cancelled.	
			During the day a Company of the 20th Royal Fusiliers came under	
			the battalion's orders. It was placed behind Battalion Head-quarters.	
			During the day the following Officers were wounded :- Captain D.S.	
			Arthur (remained at duty) 2nd Lieut R.A. Wood (before and after moving up)	
			2nd Lieut R. Stephen, Signalling Officer. 2nd Lieut J. Chapman was missing.	
	27th.		In the morning D Company was ordered to attack with the 2nd R. W.	
			Fusiliers and take the BLUE LINE. This was done the attack starting	

WAR DIARY
or
INTELLIGENCE SUMMARY.
(Erase heading not required.)

Army Form C. 2118.

Place	Date	Hour	Summary of Events and Information	Remarks and references to Appendices
			about 12.30 p.m. D Company took a pill box near JUT FARM with 14 prisoners and 2 M. Gs and a lot of stores. During the afternoon two enemy machine guns were put out of action by fire from two of D Company's Lewis Guns. These positions were held till night when the Battalion along with the 2nd R.W. Fusiliers were relieved by the 8th Yorkshire Regiment about 11 p.m. The shelling throughout till just before the relief was very heavy. Captain D.S.Arthur and Captain W. McChlery were wounded, the former for the second time. Throughout the two days the work done by the runners was highly praiseworthy. There was a great deal of shelling, but the messages were well delivered. After relief the Battalion marched back to a Camp at DICKEBUSCH.	
	28th.		The Battalion moved back in motor buses to BLARINGHEM, a small village 4 miles NORTH of AIRE.	
	30th.		Complimentary orders (See Appendix IV) were received from the Army	

Army Form C. 2118.

WAR DIARY
or
INTELLIGENCE SUMMARY.
(Erase heading not required.)

Instructions regarding War Diaries and Intelligence Summaries are contained in F. S. Regs., Part II. and the Staff Manual respectively. Title pages will be prepared in manuscript.

Place	Date	Hour	Summary of Events and Information	Remarks and references to Appendices
			Army Corps and Divisional Commanders. Information was received that the Field - Marshall Commanding - in - Chief would inspect the Division on 1st or 2nd October.	
			CASUALTIES DURING MONTH.	
			Officers :- 2/Lt. A.S. Collins died of wounds 25/9/17.	
			" P. Binnie killed in action " "	
			" R. Stephen wounded 26/9/17.	
			" H.A. Wood " " "	
			" D. Chapman missing " "	
			Capt. D.S. Arthur wounded 27/9/17.	
			" W. McOnery " " "	
			2/Lt. A.R. McGregor " (Shell shock) 27/9/17.	
			Other Ranks:- Killed in action 28	
			Wounded 119	
			Missing 52	
			Reinforcement /	

A6945 Wt. W14422/M160 350,000 12/16 D. D. & L. Forms/C./2118/14.

Army Form C. 2118.

WAR DIARY
or
INTELLIGENCE SUMMARY.
(Erase heading not required.)

Instructions regarding War Diaries and Intelligence Summaries are contained in F. S. Regs., Part II. and the Staff Manual respectively. Title pages will be prepared in manuscript.

Place	Date	Hour	Summary of Events and Information	Remarks and references to Appendices
			Reinforcement received during Month :—	
			Officers. Other Ranks.	
			Hon. Lieut & Q.M. Brown.	
			2/Lieut. J.H. Smith. 144.	
			" J.H. McPherson.	
			Strength of Battalion :—	
			Officers . . . 33	
			Other Ranks . . . 803	
			Hugh B. Spens Lieut.–Col.	
			Commanding 5th Scottish Rifles.	

5/ S.R. 19/33   Army Form C. 2118.

This copy for
Brigade

WAR DIARY
or
INTELLIGENCE SUMMARY.
(Erase heading not required.)

Army Form C. 2118.   Vol 36

Place	Date	Hour	Summary of Events and Information	Remarks and references to Appendices
			5/ Scottish Rifles	October 1914
	1 & 2	5h	The Battalion remained at BLARINGHEM, having had carried out training	
			Lunches and Ranges were being prepared when orders were received to move. At the 3rd October the 10th Infantry Brigade was inspected by	
			Sir Douglas Haig. Field Marshal Commanding in Chief. The Commander in Chief Personal the Artillery under Kitson ax	
			No 2031PM Lieut W. Gardiner.	
			No 2484 Pte (N. Noills)	
			of the Battalion. The Commander in Chief expressed his entire satisfaction with the turn out.	Appendix I
	4th		On the 4th October. Orders were received that the Brigade would move to TILQUES, leaving area	
			The Battalion had Reveille at 2.30 a.m. and moved off at 5 a.m. and marched to ZAUDAUSQUES and ROCQUINGHEM, – ARQUES – LONGUENESSE – MISQUES, a distance of about 14 miles arriving there at 12 noon The billets here were fair.	
	5th		Orders received about 2 a.m. that the Division was transferred from	37⊘ 11sheet

Army Form C. 2118.

WAR DIARY
or
INTELLIGENCE SUMMARY.
(Erase heading not required.)

Instructions regarding War Diaries and Intelligence Summaries are contained in F. S. Regs., Part II. and the Staff Manual respectively. Title pages will be prepared in manuscript.

Place	Date	Hour	Summary of Events and Information	Remarks and references to Appendices
2/ Scottish Rifles			October 1914	
			7th to 8th Corps and that the Division should move to Cassel area.	
			BAILLEUL The Transport moved off at 1.20 AM and came by road staying one night at BURINGHEM. The Battalion entrained at NISERNES at 5.15 pm and detrained at BAILLEUL about midnight.	
	7th		The Battalion arrived at Camp B. KORTEPYP about ½ mile E of BAILLEUL at 2 AM. The Second in Command (Major Scott) and Company Commanders reconnoitred the left sub-sector of the line held by the 11th Division.	
	8th		Alarm received from 11th Corps that enemy attacking. The Battalion moved to the good work N of Bob on 27th and 28th September. The Battalion moved into support see Appendix II at dot on 25th and 26th September. The 9th K.R.R.C. 42nd Coy Bde 14th Division K.S.L.I. MESSINES RIDGE relieving the 9th K.R.R.C. 42nd Coy Bde 14th Division K.S.L.I. During the Battalion moved into the front line and relieved the 5th K.S.L.I. The 1st Royal Welsh Fusiliers took over the Support line. The trenches were found in a very poor state of repair and the battalion was happy doing strong doing repairs and laying stones heads ?c. Loads of R.E. Material had to be carried up.	
	12th		The Battalion moved back into support and the 1st Royal Welsh Fusiliers	

A6945 Wt. W1422/M1160 350,000 12/16 D. D. & L. Forms/C./2118/14.

WAR DIARY
or
INTELLIGENCE SUMMARY

Army Form C. 2118.

Place	Date	Hour	Summary of Events and Information	Remarks and references to Appendices
5/ Scottish Rifles			October 1917	
	14th		went into the front line. "A" Company under 2nd Lieut. Grant was placed at the disposal of the 2nd R.W.F. for carrying R.E. material also for tactical purposes. Great improvements were made in the support line and advice dugouts made. The Battalion was relieved by the 9th H.L.I. and moved back to SHANKILL CAMP, NEUVE EGLISE. Warning order received to be prepared to move to ANZAC CORPS.	
	15th		Orders received to relieve the 2nd A. & S.H. in the area of the 2nd ANZAC CORPS in a camp about ½ mile W. of S. in St JEAN, N.E. of YPRES	
	16th		The Battalion entrained at 12 noon and detrained at KRUISSTRAAT about 5pm. The Battalion worked under the 2nd Canadian Railway Troops making a Light Railway. The work was fairly hard and tiring. The area in which the camp was situated was heavily shelled at night and on the afternoon of the 17th the area was even shelled. One shell alighted in a tent killing of the pieces and scattering body parts to the occupants of the tent were all sent on leave at the same.	
	18th to 26th		The Battalion moved back about 2 miles to a camp about ½ mile N.W. of the ASYLUM YPRES. The 2nd ANZAC CORPS relieved by a CANADIAN CORPS. Message from Brigade with the following information :- The Corps Commander has awarded the following decoration to the under-mentioned N.C.O's and men :-	

Army Form C. 2118.

WAR DIARY
or
INTELLIGENCE SUMMARY.
(Erase heading not required.)

Instructions regarding War Diaries and Intelligence Summaries are contained in F. S. Regs., Part II. and the Staff Manual respectively. Title pages will be prepared in manuscript.

5/ Scottish Rifles   October 1917

Place	Date	Hour	Summary of Events and Information	Remarks and references to Appendices
			MILITARY MEDAL	
			No 200086 Sgt. R.W. Edmiston	
			240277 Sgt. L.J. Stewart	
			202323 Cpl. W. Carle	
			22004 " G. Trant	
			200180 Sgt. G. Kratz	
			201113 Cpl. W. McCulloch	
			200545 Sgt. J. Hay	
			201515 Cpl. Jas. Anderson	
			240101 " W. Hill	
			200930 " W. McLeod	
			200116 " J.R. Martin	
			200896 " G. De Emba	
			200855 " W. Gillespie	
			The Corps, Divisional and Brigade Commanders sent their congratulations.	
			These medals were given for distinguished conduct on 26th/28th September 1917.	
	21st		Under orders received to join the 33/Division.	
	22nd		The Battalion was relieved by the 5th Cameron Battalion. It entrained at 12 noon on YPRES ASYLUM KRUISSTRAAT Road and detrained at NEUVE EGLISE and moved into ALDERSHOT CAMP there, the Battalion remained here training as far as the ground would allow. Musketry and wiring were practised by all Companies.	
	30th		The Battalion relieved the 2nd H. & S. H. on the left sub sector of the Division on the front line.	

Army Form C. 2118.

WAR DIARY
or
INTELLIGENCE SUMMARY.
(Erase heading not required.)

Place	Date	Hour	Summary of Events and Information	Remarks and references to Appendices
5/ Scottish Rifles	October 1917			
	3/10		Message received from Brigade with the following information:- the Field Marshal Commanding in Chief has awarded the Military Cross for distinguished conduct in the field on 26th September 1917. - to Capt. D. S. Arthur and 2/Lieut. D. N. Maclachlan Casualties during the month Officers Other Ranks Nil 6 Reinforcements received during month Capt. W. A. Parker " C. E. Grant Lieut. R. J. Colville 142 " J. A. Sutton 2/Lieut. H. Kerr " A. J. Hopin Strength of Battalion Officers 36 Other Ranks 844	

A. J. B. Speir
LIEUT. COLONEL,
COMMANDING 5th BATT. SCOTTISH RIFLES.

5 Scottish Rifles
Army Form C. 2118.

WAR DIARY
or
INTELLIGENCE SUMMARY.
(Erase heading not required.)

NOVEMBER 1917

Place	Date	Hour	Summary of Events and Information	Remarks and references to Appendices
5/Scottish Rifles	2nd		Orders received that the 2nd Royal Welsh Fusiliers would relieve the Battalion 3rd instant and the Battalion would move back into Support Trenches on THE MESSINES RIDGE.	
	3rd		The Battalion was relieved by the 2/R.W.F. and moved into Support. It rained here for three days. Efforts were made and 200 men worked nightly digging a support line. 50 yards were completed nightly.	
	5th		Telegram received from 5th Reserve Bn. Scottish Rifles on occasion of their 1st anniversary of the Battalion landing in France. See App I	
			Letter from Lord Provost & Lord Lieutenant of the County of the City of Glasgow on his Lordship's office, extending thanks for the great work of the Battalion.	See App II
	7th		The Battalion was relieved by the 16th K.R.R.C. and moved back to Camp "B" KORTEPYP	
5th to 13th			The Battalion remained at KORTEPYP cleaning and training so far as the ground and weather permits permitted.	
	13th		The Battalion moved to STRAZEELE.	
	14th		The Battalion moved by bus to YPRES and thence by road to near POTIJZE. Here a sad affair took place on the night of the 18th. A shell landed in "C Coy." Officers tent killing Capt. L.R.W. Whitlock M.C. and wounding all his Platoon Commanders. Capt. Whitlock came out as a Sergeant with the Battalion in 1914.	
	17th			
	19th		The Battalion moved into LANCER CAMP POTIJZE	
	20th 2.30		The Battalion relieved the 1/ Wiltshire Regiment in RIGHT SUPPORT SUBSECTOR behind PASSCHENDAELE. The ground was in a dreadful state of mud and shell holes.	

Army Form C. 2118.

WAR DIARY
or
INTELLIGENCE SUMMARY.
(Erase heading not required.)

Place	Date	Hour	Summary of Events and Information	Remarks and references to Appendices
5/Scottish Rifles			NOVEMBER 1917	
			Note. The Battalion Headquarters were in a small PILL BOX 2'9" high and Aid Post was a tarpaulin lean-to.	
	24th		The Battalion relieved the 4th Kings in the RIGHT FRONT SUB SECTOR. It rained shell holes and small trenches. Rations and hot food were taken up nightly under heavy shell fire.	
	27th		The Battalion was relieved by the 2nd Royal Fusiliers and moved back into SUPPORT	
	29th		Working parties of 200 men were out from 6.30 A.M. to 12.30 P.M. carrying R.E. material and digging a Communication Trench to the front line. The Battalion (less "C" Coy under 2nd Lieut. Bailie) was relieved by the 2nd Worcesters Regiment and moved back to POTIJZE. "C" Coy relieved a company of the 2nd R.W.F. in the LEFT FRONT SUB SECTOR. This Company of the 2/R.W.F. had gone in a day earlier owing to heavy casualties.	
	30th		The Battalion (less "C" Company) entrained at ST JEAN, detrained at BRANDHOEK and marched to TORONTO CAMP.	
			Reinforcements received during month	
			2nd Lieut. L.t. G. Barr	
			" C. C. Bergne	
			" B. J. Taylor	
			Lieut. K.W. Begg	
			Casualties	
			16 other ranks	

WAR DIARY or INTELLIGENCE SUMMARY

NOVEMBER 1917

5/7 Scottish Rifles

Casualties during month

2nd Lieut. C.H. Smith .... Wounded 3/11/17
Lieut. L.R. Colville .... Wounded (gas) 5/11/17
Capt. L.R.W. Walcot, M.C. .... Killed in action 18/11/17
2nd Lieut. A.H. Sime .... Wounded 18/11/17
" J.C.G. Barr .... "
" K.J. Napier .... "
Capt. L.J. Evans, R.A.M.C. .... Wounded (gas) 5/11/17

Other ranks
Killed in action 19
Wounded 30
Wounded (gas) 16
Wounded (at duty) 5

Strength of Battalion
Officers 32
Other Ranks 780

[signed] Lieut. Colonel
Commanding 5/7 Scottish Rifles

Army Form C. 2118.

WAR DIARY
or
INTELLIGENCE SUMMARY.
(Erase heading not required.)

1/5 Scottish Rifles

Place	Date	Hour	Summary of Events and Information DECEMBER 1917	Remarks and references to Appendices
	1st Dec.		5TH SCOTTISH RIFLES "C" Company which had been attached to the 2nd Royal Scots Fusiliers rejoined	
	2nd to 5th Dec.		The Battn. remained at TORONTO CAMP cleaning and training as far as the ground would permit	
	6th Dec.		The Battn. moved from TORONTO CAMP BRANDHOEK to POTIJZE and took over the Camp vacated by the 16th K.R.R.C.	
	7th to 10th Dec.		Working parties had to be supplied daily, the whole battalion being employed on the work, the work consisted chiefly in repairing and making light railways and a new plank road, the shelling on both being very heavy at times, the area in which the camp was situated was bombed by day and by night but the battalion luckily suffered no casualties	
	11th to 26th Dec.		The Battalion was relieved by the 4th Yorkshire Regt and entrained at ST. JEAN & detrained at ABEELE and marched into an area near WATOU. The officers	

WAR DIARY or INTELLIGENCE SUMMARY

Army Form C. 2118.

Place	Date	Hour	Summary of Events and Information	Remarks and references to Appendices
	20th Dec		accommodation was poor and the men had the usual thing. The training commenced on the usual lines. Cinema was started and arrangements were being made for a photography cluster for the men when orders were received for the Battn to proceed to ST JEAN. Lieut Col A.A. KENNEDY, D.S.O, T.D assumed command of the Battalion	
	21st to 26th Dec		The Battn. less transport, Lewis Gun class, Bombing class and a few details (1 Off 150 O.R) entrained at ABEELE and detrained at ST JEAN and relieved the 2nd Worcestershire Regt at ENGLISH FARM CAMP. Working parties (3 Coys) were supplied daily to assist the 490th and 507 R.E and 22nd D.L.I (Pioneers) in making and repairing PANET ROAD from KANSAS CROSS to SEINE. The area was 'rouché' our night and a few shells fell near the Battn suffered no casualties.	
	27th Dec		The Battn. entrained at ST JEAN and detrained at ABEELE and marched back to billets previously occupied	

Army Form C. 2118.

WAR DIARY
or
INTELLIGENCE SUMMARY.
(Erase heading not required.)

Instructions regarding War Diaries and Intelligence Summaries are contained in F. S. Regs., Part II. and the Staff Manual respectively. Title pages will be prepared in manuscript.

Place	Date	Hour	Summary of Events and Information	Remarks and references to Appendices
In the WATOU AREA	28th to 31st Dec		Training carried out on the usual lines. All ranks in the Battalion had their usual Box Respirators tested with tear attack and a clear change arrangements completed for usual New Year dinner. Orders received that the Battn. will move forward again on the 3rd Janry. 1918. Reinforcements received during the month. OTHER RANKS 123 OFFICERS Lt Col A.A. KENNEDY D.S.O. T.D. LIEUT A.F. STRUTHERS " S.L. BRAND-CROMBIE " A.M. KIRKWOOD 2/LIEUT T.S. WHYTE " R. DICK " T.C. CUTHBERTSON " G.H. YOUNG " D.M. FORD " C.S. McDONALD " D. McGREGOR	

Army Form C. 2118.

WAR DIARY
or
INTELLIGENCE SUMMARY.
(Erase heading not required.)

5th Scottish Rifles.   Summary of Events and Information   January, 1918.

Place	Date	Hour	Summary of Events and Information	Remarks and references to Appendices
	1		The Battalion remained in Billets in WATOU Area. The day was observed as a holiday a special dinner being provided for the men.	
	2		Battalion resumed training.	
	3		Moved from WATOU Area to ERIE CAMP, BRANDHOEK, entraining at ABEELE and completing journey by rail.	
	4/15		Marched from BRANDHOEK to ST JEAN CAMP, YPRES - Route via VLAMERTINGHE. Took over camp vacated by Northumberland Fusiliers. Battalion while in this camp provided working parties to R.E. work consisting of making read for light railways and laying rails.	
	16		Battalion moved into support at HAMBURG via Judah Track relieving 1st Middlesex Regt.	
	17		Relieved 4th Suffolks Regt. in Right Front Sector.	
	19		Relieved by 2nd Worcesters in line and moved by light railway from LOW FARM JUNCTION to ST LAWRENCE CAMP, BRANDHOEK vacated by 9th H.L.I.	
	20/22		Cleaning up and re-equiping was carried on during stay in this camp.	
	23		Entrained on light railway at BRANDHOEK Station and detrained at LOW FARM thence by Judah Track to right front sector relieving the 4th Kings Regt. there.	
	25		Relieved by 2nd Worcester Regt in line and entraining on light railway at LOW FARM moved back to YPRES.	
	26		Billeted in cellars in YPRES.	
	27/			

Army Form C. 2118.

WAR DIARY
or
INTELLIGENCE SUMMARY.
(Erase heading not required.)

Instructions regarding War Diaries and Intelligence Summaries are contained in F.S. Regs., Part II. and the Staff Manual respectively. Title pages will be prepared in manuscript.

Place	Date	Hour	Summary of Events and Information	Remarks and references to Appendices
			January, 1918.	
			5th Scottish Rifles.	
	27		Entrained at ST JEAN STATION and moved back by train to ST OMER. Detrained there and marched to TATINGHEM.	
	28		Cleaning up, re-equipment and inspections were gone on with during the day.	
	29		Same work carried on. Brig.General C.MAYNE, D.S.O. inspected billets.	
	30/31		Training was started in the forenoon and carried on till 12-30 p.m. Specialist training and games were carried on in the afternoon. Officers Riding Class at 3.30 p.m.	

The following Honors appeared in New Year List :-

D.S.O.
Major H.B.Spens.
Mentioned in Despatches.
Major H.B.Spens
Capt K.Ashby Brown (K in A.)
240026 R.Q.M.S. Ronshaw, H.
200008 Sgt Wallace, R.B. (K in A.)
Increase in Pay.
Hon.Capt. & Quartermaster J.Brown.

Casualties during month.

Other Ranks :- Wounded 5. Killed in Action 3.
Officers :- Nil.

Reinforcement received during month :-

Officers.
Lieut. Hogarth, W.
Lieut. Napier, C.H.
2/Lt. Smith, W.H.
Other Ranks.
37

Army Form C. 2118.

WAR DIARY
or
INTELLIGENCE SUMMARY.

(*Erase heading not required.*)

Place	Date	Hour	Summary of Events and Information	Remarks and references to Appendices
			Strength of Battalion.	
			Officers 42	
			Other Ranks. 945.	
			[signature]	
			Lieut-Col.	
			Commanding 5th Scottish Rifles.	

Instructions regarding War Diaries and Intelligence Summaries are contained in F. S. Regs., Part II. and the Staff Manual respectively. Title pages will be prepared in manuscript.

Army Form C. 2118.

WAR DIARY
or
INTELLIGENCE SUMMARY.
(Erase heading not required.)

5TH SCOTTISH RIFLES.　　Summary of Events and Information　　FEBRUARY, 1918.

Place	Date	Hour	Summary of Events and Information	Remarks and references to Appendices
	1/14		Battalion carried on with training in the forenoons. Training area being used on all occasions. Afternoons were occupied in specialist training and recreation. The range was good.	
	15		A Transport Inspection was held on this date. The Battalion Transport was commanded by Brig. General MAYNE, D.S.O.	
	16		Brigade Pack Mule Loading and Vehicle Competition won by this unit.	
	17		Major General PINNEY, C.B., presented medal ribands to eight Other Ranks on Training ground :- 240277 Sgt. J.F. Stewart. 200545 " T. Hay. 240101 L/Cpl. W. Hill. 200176 " J.R. Martin. 200896 " E. DeCunha. 200851 " W. Gillespie. 202326 Rfm. W. Coull. 201515 " W. Andersen. Church parade followed immediately after.	
	18		Battalion attended Demonstration of Low Flying Aeroplane followed by cloud gas demonstration. Baths at ST OMER were also attended.	
			Transport (1st Line) moved by road to Forward Area.	
	20		Battalion moved by train to POTIJZE, entraining at WIZERNES and detraining at YPRES, thence to MAIDEN CAMP.	
	21		Battalion relieved the 4th East Yorks Regiment in the RIGHT SUB-SECTOR of Front Line. Headquarters at INDIGO. Moved via light railway to BORRY FARM thence by JUDAH TRACK to line.	

Army Form C. 2118.

WAR DIARY
or
INTELLIGENCE SUMMARY.
(Erase heading not required.)

Instructions regarding War Diaries and Intelligence Summaries are contained in F.S. Regs., Part II. and the Staff Manual respectively. Title pages will be prepared in manuscript.

Place	Date	Hour	Summary of Events and Information	Remarks and references to Appendices
5th SCOTTISH RIFLES.			FEBRUARY, 1918.	
	21		Immediately on relief two exposed forward posts on the right front Company were raided by the enemy. Casualties :- Killed. 3 Wounded. 3 Missing. 13	
	23		An inter company relief took place, 2 Companies in Support moving into line and other two moving into support.	
	25		Battalion was relieved in the line by the 2nd Argyll and Sutherland Highlanders. Moved out via JUDAH TRACK to BORRY FARM thence by light railway to POTIJZE. Accommodated in MAIDEN CAMP.	
	26		Bathing took place in YPRES.	
	27		All companies moved out at least 90 strong for work on Army Battle Zone.	
	28		Demonstration of Organisation of Shell Hole Defences by Brigade Major attended by Officers and N.C.Os. Specialist Training carried on. Casualties during month. Officers. Killed. Nil. Other Ranks. Wounded 3 " at duty. 13 Missing. 3 Reinforcements received during month. Officers 2/Lieut R.S.Hamilton. Other Ranks. 41 Strength of Battalion. Officers 40 Other Ranks. 907.	

Hugh B Spens Major.
5th Scottish Rifles.

1/5 Scottish Rifle
Army Form C. 2118.
Vol 44

42-0
2 sheet

WAR DIARY
or
INTELLIGENCE SUMMARY.
(Erase heading not required.)

5TH SCOTTISH RIFLES.   Summary of Events and Information   **MARCH, 1918.**

Place	Date	Hour	Summary of Events and Information	Remarks and references to Appendices
1918. March	1st.		Battalion moved into the Front Line relieving the 2nd Argyll & Sutherland Highlanders in the Right Sub-Sector Left Brigade.	
	5th		Battalion was relieved by the 2nd Argyll & Sutherland Highlanders and moved to Malden Camp, YPRES.	
	9th		Battalion moved into Right Support relieving the 1st Middlesex Regiment at IRKSOME.	
	10/15		While in Support at IRKSOME Battalion supplied carrying parties to the 1st Cameronians and the 1st Queens Regiment in the Front Line. Two Companies were held in readiness for counter attacking purposes.	
	15		Battalion was relieved by 2nd Argyll and Sutherland Highlanders and moved back to WHITBY CAMP, YPRES.	
	17/20		Battalion supplied working parties to R.E. on Battle Zone and Divisional Reserve Lines.	
	19th		Owing to enemy activity shelling back areas the Battalion moved from WHITBY CAMP, YPRES to ST LAWRENCE CAMP, BRANDHOEK by rail.	
	21st		Battalion relieved 1st Middlesex Regiment in Front Line Right Front Sub-Sector Left Brigade at INDIGO entraining at BRANDHOEK Light Railway Station and detraining at BORRY FARM. All the way Gas Shells were falling and Box Respirators were worn. No casualties.	
	24th		An inter-company relief was carried out. "C" Company from HAALEN and "D" Company from HILLSIDE relieved "A" and "B" Companies in the Front Line. During this tour two Officer Patrols were sent out nightly. Enemy Posts were found but no identifications were got. Work on the posts was carried out.	

Army Form C. 2118.

WAR DIARY
or
INTELLIGENCE SUMMARY.
(Erase heading not required.)

Instructions regarding War Diaries and Intelligence Summaries are contained in F. S. Regs., Part II. and the Staff Manual respectively. Title pages will be prepared in manuscript.

Place	Date	Hour	Summary of Events and Information	Remarks and references to Appendices
			5TH SCOTTISH RIFLES. **MARCH, 1918.**	
1918. March	27th		Battalion was relieved by the 2nd Argyll & Sutherland Highlanders and proceeded by Light Railway to BRANDHOEK where it was accommodated in TORONTO WEST CAMP.	
	29th		All Companies fired on the range.	
	28/31		Little training was done as the Battalion supplied working parties to the R.E. on Battle Zone and Divisional Reserve Line and also to the Camp Commandant at BRANDHOEK.	
	31st.		Commanding Officer and Company Commanders reconnoitred new portion of the Line which the Battalion will take over on the night 2nd/3rd April. Orders received that Battalion would stand by ready to move by Bus on one hour's notice to an unknown destination.	

Reinforcements received during month.
    Officers.
      Lt. T.O.Thorburn.
      Lt. J.B.L.Loudon.
      2/Lt. F. Sunter.

Casualties during month.
                                Other Ranks.
    Killed in action.   9
    Wounded   26
    Wounded (Gas)   11
  Nil.   123.

Strength of Battalion.
    Other Ranks.   970.
    Officers.   39.

A. Hyslop. Lt. Col.
Cmdg. 5th Scottish Rifles.

19th Brigade.

33rd Division.

1/5th BATTALION

CAMERONIANS (Scottish Rifles)

APRIL 1918.

War Diary

19/33

5th Scottish Rifles

April, 1918.

1st. The Battalion moved by bus during the night of 31st March/1st April to LIENCOURT.

2nd,3rd,4th. The Battalion stayed at LIENCOURT. Training was carried on, particular attention being paid to rapid fire on the range.

5th. The Battalion marched to Y Camp at DUISANS.

7th. The Battalion marched back to LIENCOURT

8th to 9th. Training was continued as before.

10th. The Battalion marched to AUBIGNY

11th. The Battalion moved by train to CAESTRE and thence by bus and march to METEREN. outposts were put out. The Brigade was in Corps Reserve.

12th. About 2.30 p.m. orders were received (S.B.40) to move to a position of readiness about Appendix No. 1 1500 yards N.E. of METEREN ready to occupy a line from there to METEREN. The Queens were taking up a position on the South of METEREN. The line to be occupied by the Battalion was being dug by 18th Middlesex Pioneers and some R.E. Companies. The Battalion moved off through METEREN and three towards its/

War Diary

5th Scottish Rifles

April, 1918.

12th — Its position of readiness in artillery formation. Patrols were sent out to the south who got in touch with the troops holding a line to the South of BAILLEUL and also the enemy. A platoon from (No. 13 Platoon) was established near STEAM MILL (X 24 c 0.2. Sheet 27) O.C. 5th Scottish Rifles arranged with O.C. 18th Middlesex that the latter should hold the southern part of the line about the METEREN – BAILLEUL Road but at 6 p.m. orders were received — the order was issued at 4 p.m. but went astray — for one Company 5th Scottish Rifles to occupy a position across the main METEREN – BAILLEUL road getting in touch with the Queens on the right. "D" Coy (3 platoons) plus 1 platoon "C" Coy were then ordered up to occupy a position from about 1,000 yards due S of METEREN to athwart the METEREN – BAILLEUL road (X 22 c 5.0 – X 16 d 7.6 Sheet 27) O.C. 5th Scottish Rifles then

War Diary

5th Scottish Rifles

April 1918.

12th

then arranged with O.C. 18th Middlesex for the latter to withdraw his Companies and the Battalion occupied the line about 5 p.m. which ran N. and N.E. from the main MÉTEREN-BAILLEUL road, the line running roughly as follows :- X 22 c 5 0 — X 16 d 7 6 — X 16 d 7 9 — X 10 c 9 0 — X 11 a 4 0 (Sheet 27) The order of Coys holding the line from right to left being D Coy. one platoon C Coy, C Coy, B Coy, A Coy. A Coy had one platoon in advance at the cross-roads at X 11 a 5 0. Details of the 93rd Brigade were in B Coys line and in support of it. The line to the East of X 11 a 4 0 was held by the 255th Tunnelling Coy and 222nd Field Coy R.E. The 171st Tunnelling Coy were in Battalion Reserve. At about the same time information was received that the 22nd Corps Reinforcement Battalion were deploying from the junction of 5th Scottish Rifles and Queens X 22 c 5 0 to STEAM MILL (X 24 c 0 2) where

War Diary.

5th Scottish Rifles.

April, 1918.

12th	where they joined up with the 147th Brigade attached 34th Division. Orders were issued for No 13 Platoon to withdraw from STEAM MILL and rejoin D Company. 1 Platoon C Company still remained under O.C. D Coy's orders. The Battalion was thus holding a patch line in case of a break through at BAILLEUL where the position was observed. Battalion Headquarters were established at X 10 c 3.9 in a farm. Touch was obtained by D Coy with the Queens on the right. 18th Middlesex and 2nd N.Z. Entrenching Battalion were now in Brigade Reserve a little N of METEREN. Shortly before midnight orders were received that 171st and 255th Tunnelling Coys. were to be withdrawn. The Battalion line was then extended to X 11 c 0.9 where touch was obtained with 222nd Field Coy. By this time the details of the 93rd Brigade near the METEREN-BAILLEUL road had increased largely

War Diary

5th Scottish Rifles

April 1918

in numbers and several O.C Battalions were reported there. Instructions from Brigade were asked as to the position with regard to these details. There was little hostile and no British Artillery fire all day.

13th. The positions of D Company S of the main METEREN – BAILLEUL road were advanced forward as the result of a reconnaissance by C.O and C.oy Cmdrs in the early morning. Arrangements were made with O.C. Battalions 93rd Brigade details for them to occupy support positions. The enemy were reported about 7.35am by 1st Queens to have broken through 22nd Corps Reinforcement Battalion on their left but this report was incorrect. During the morning the enemy attacked the 1st Queens on our right and their centre was reported driven in. Patrols were sent out by D.C.oy and a German Officers killed and identification obtained by Corporal McLeod, M.M. B Echelon during the morning moved forward and took up a position S of METEREN in rear of the left of 1st Queens and right of 5th Scottish Rifles. There was intermittent shelling of the front

War Diary

5th Scottish Rifles.   April, 1918

13th	Front line during the morning. About noon 3 British Batteries came into action near Battalion Headquarters and close touch was kept with them. At 3.15 p.m. enemy were reported by a patrol massing on our front and hostile artillery activity increased greatly also Machine Gun fire. The forward posts were heavily bombarded and the rest of the Battalion line was also shelled. About 7 p.m. the left posts of the 1st Queens and right posts of the XXII Corps Reinforcement Batln were driven in and our two right posts were carried back with them. During this fighting one post commander close to where the line had been driven in killed 12 Germans by the fire of his section and took two prisoners himself at the point of the bayonet. The line was re-established with our right about X.22.a 2.2. where it got touch with XXII Corps Reinforcement Battalion and 5th Scottish Rifles B Echelon and through them with 1st Queens.

War Diary

5th Scottish Rifles

April, 1918

13th

At 8.7 p.m. 19th Infantry Brigade placed B Battalion 5th Scottish Rifles under orders of O.C. Orders to strengthen our line S. of METEREN were also received. ½ Company 18th Middlesex were placed under the orders of O.C. 5th Scottish Rifles. Information was also urgently asked for from Battalion and O.C. D Company, Captain Kirkwood, by Brigade as to KX 11 Corps Battalion's position. They were reported to be on original position except on right where they had fallen back to about X 22 a 2 2. Orders were issued for Major Scott and Captain Kirkwood to re-arrange the line S of METEREN. Orders were issued to endeavour to push in again to X 22 C 4.0 but as the Queens left had fallen back this was not possible. Dispositions were reported to 19th Infantry Brigade. 2 Platoons 18th Middlesex reinforced D Coy who had had the [illegible] casualties. South of the METEREN - BAILLEUL road 93rd Brigade details formed

a/

War Diary

5th Scottish Rifles   April 1918.

13th   a support line in touch with B Echelon on the right and with their
       left about the main BAILLEUL - METEREN road. At the
       close of the day a congratulatory message was received by G.O.C.
       Brigade from G.H.Q., Army, and Corps through Division.

                                                         Appendix No 2.

14th   The position of our right as stated by O.C. D Coy. on the 13th was on the
       early morning and reported to the Brigade. During the morning
       the enemy began to mass troops opposite our right. The 22nd Corps
       Reinforcement Battalion gave way during the day and D Coy by rifle and
       Lewis Gun fire held up the enemy's advance inflicting substantial losses.
       2nd N.Z. Entrenching Battalion were pushed forward by the Brigade to occupy
       the line of the main METEREN - BAILLEUL road east from the sunken lane
       held by D Coy and endeavour to re-establish the position at dark. The
       enemy also attacked 1st Queens on our right. 22nd Corps Battalion were
       rallied and reformed as far as possible on our line. D Coy held its
       line on the right of the sunken all day and suffered very heavy casualties

War Diary

5th Scottish Rifles

April 1918.

14th/15th During the night and early morning the Battalion was relieved by the 5th Yorks Battalion. Details of 93rd Brigade, 2 Platoons 18th Middlesex and 222nd Field Coy were relieved with the Battalion. The Battalion moved back to FONTAIN HOEK in close support. The C.O. about 11.30 a.m. on reporting his dispositions at Headquarters was informed that the Battalion would relieve the 1st Cameronians S.W. of METEREN that night. 1st Cameronians had attached to them 1 Coy N.Z. Entrenching Battalion. The 1st Cameronians were visited and all arrangements made. Later the Battalion was ordered to also relieve 1 Coy 4th Kings on left of 1st Cameronians, this Coy had a 5th Platoon attached to it. The Battalion were disposed as follows :— Right Coy D less 1 Platoon. Right Centre B. 2/L Centre A. Left Coy C 1 Platoon D Coy in Battalion reserve. 4th Australian Battalion on right. 4th Kings on left.

15th/16th The relief was carried out during the night. The front attended from /

War Diary

5th Scottish Rifles — April 1918

15th/16th	from about X 25 a 0 0 – X 14 c 3 4 (approximately) The front held by the Battalion was a very wide one and it was impossible to keep any reserve on hand but owing to the situation it was necessary for the Battalion to be ordered to hold this front. In the morning the Battalion received orders to relieve with the reserve platoon some posts held by the R E (2 sections 11th Field Coy) in X 19 b and X 20 a near Battalion Headquarters which were about X 13 c 8 8. Before this relief was carried out an attack developed and the two sections R E stayed on. During the day the enemy heavily attacked the Battalion on our left (4th Kings) and the troops on their left and our left Coy (C Coy) METEREN was taken and the flank of the 4th Kings turned with the result that they were forced to form a defensive flank. The left flank of C Coy was slightly refused to keep in touch with the right Coy of the 4th Kings. Otherwise no ground was lost.

War Diary

5th Scottish Rifles   April, 1918

15th/16th	lost E Coy beat off repeated attacks, inflicting very heavy losses on the enemy. A Coy was also attacked at one time but beat it off easily. The other two Coys had good targets all day and had good shooting at them. The 1 Platoon of D Coy in reserve and 2 sections of 11th Field Coy RE were sent up to assist 4th Kings. No 15 Platoon were used to fill a gap on the Kings right and came under orders of O.C. C Coy while the 2 sections of 11th Field Coy under Lt FEARY made a most gallant and successful counter attack. After METEREN was taken the line was troubled by enfilade Machine Gun fire from immediately W of METEREN and about the Church. There was also heavy shelling from time to time. The 133rd French Division moved up in support and liaison was obtained with 32nd Chasseurs. The O.C. 32nd Chasseurs gave a platoon to support 4th Kings on being asked for it. Close liaison was also obtained with our own and the French Artillery who used the Battalions Observation Post - a barn at Headquarters - and effective Artillery support obtained. At 6.30 pm the French received orders to attack at 6 p.m. They moved forward and the Battalion

War Diary

5th Scottish Rifles

April, 1918.

15th/16th Battalion Intelligence Officer (Lt W Hogarth) and 2 runners went forward with them, but owing to darkness no attack was made. In the evening the 4th Australian Battalion on our right carried out a minor operation to advance the line. The operation was successful to begin with but latterly owing to casualties they had to retire and O.C. D Coy filled in a gap between him and 4th Australian Battalion with his support platoon. Some Germans were captured by him while doing so.
Information was received during the evening that the Battalion was to be relieved that night by 1st Australian Battalion. It was arranged reliefs should take place just before dawn, the Australians digging further posts first covered by us. Later it turned out the French went to relieve the left of C Coy N of the METEREN-BECK.

16th/17th On the night owing to the boundaries of 1st and 4th Australian Battalions being

War Diary.

5th Scottish Rifles.   April, 1918

16th/17th	Found it was impossible to relieve D Coy (3 platoons) The relief of the Battalion was completed just about dawn, and the Battalion moved back to the II Army Signalling School near MT DES CATS. Owing to shelling above the Battalion moved into fields near and bivouacked, most of the men found cover in barns. D Coy had a splendid day with the Australians. The enemy attacked repeatedly but were beaten off well away from our lines by rifle and Lewis Gun fire. Splendid targets were obtained. One Lewis Gun team having no rations, knocked out a German ration party and secured views. A letter from O.C. 1st Australian Battalion was received praising the work of D Coy (copy appended) Appendix No. 3 Throughout the whole of the above operations the lessons learned were:- (1) Rifle and Lewis Gun fire will beat off attacks and having no rapid fire is essential. (2) Troops that stick to their posts do not suffer heavy casualties and will not be driven back.
18th	D Coy rejoined the Battalion in the early morning. Orders were received for the Brigade

War Diary

5th Scottish Rifles.   April, 1918.

18th	Brigade to go into the line again that night but this was cancelled.
19th	The Battalion moved to a position of readiness N of ST JANS CAPPEL and dug in here in a wood. The Brigade came under the orders of the 34th Division. Orders were received for the Battalion to relieve the 4th Duke of Wellington's Regiment in support (Battalion Headquarters ST JANS CAPPEL) and all arrangements were made for the relief. Later these orders were cancelled and the Battalion received orders to relieve the 2nd Argyll and Sutherland Highlanders on the line S of SCHAEXKEN. The Battalion only relieved 1 Coy of 2nd Argyll & Sutherland Highlanders here together with some details 10th Corps School Battalion and 9th Corps Cyclists. Battalion Headquarters was established in a farm. The Battalion was disposed in depth. A Coy front line, B Coy support line D Coy reserve line C Coy for counter attack near Battalion Headquarters. Information was received that the Battalion would be relieved the following night by a Battalion of the 32nd Regiment of French Infantry

20/

War Diary

5th Scottish Rifles

April 1918.

20th A reconnoitring party came up from 321st Regiment French Infantry and arrangements were made for the relief of the Battalion to be carried out in the early morning of the 21st. The day passed very quietly.

21st The Battalion was relieved by a Battalion of the 321st Regiment of French Infantry. This Battalion relieved the whole Brigade. 1 Coy relieving our A Coy, 1 Coy the front line of the Cameronians and 1 Coy all supports and reserves. The Battalion moved back to W of Mt DES CATS where it had breakfasts. Later in the day the Battalion moved back to 5 of CASSEL being quartered in an Aerodrome.

21st/28th Training was carried on. Musketry was again paid particular attention to — rapid fire.

29th Orders received at 3.45 AM that Brigade would move to RACQUINGHEM. These orders were cancelled at 10 AM and Battalion remained at Aerodrome. Training was resumed.

30th Massed Pipe Bands 1st Battalion The Cameronians, 2nd Argyll & Sutherland Highlanders, 9th Highland Light Infantry and 5th Scottish Rifles Played at 9th H.L.I. Bde Sports.

War Diary

5th Scottish Rifles   April 1918.

30th	Headquarters at 5/6 m.

Casualties during month.

— Officers —   — Other Ranks —

Lt. J.B.L. London	Killed in action 13.4.18.	Killed	26
Lt. J.O. Thorburn	do	Wounded	86
Lt. A.O.C. Fryer	do 14.4.18	Wounded and missing	1
2/Lt. D. McGregor	wounded 14.4.18	Missing	17
2/Lt. G.H. Young	do 16.4.18	Wounded at duty	3
Lt. R. Wilson	do do		
2/Lt. D.H. Ford	do 19.4.18		
2/Lt. C.G. Cheyne	missing 14.4.18		
2/Lt. W. McCulloch	to hospital NYD shell shock 14.4.18		

Reinforcements received.

Officers :- Lt. A.O.C. Fryer   2/Lt. R.L.C. Yorret   2/Lt. Hibbert
           Lt. H. Blair   2/Lt. G. Fraser
           Lt. R. Wilson   2/Lt. R.W. McDougall

Other Ranks :- 131

Strength of Battalion.

Officers   38
Other Ranks   921

Hy. B. Spens   Lt. Col.
Cmdg. 5th Scottish Rifles.

Copy.   C.B.40.

5th S.R.
----

1. Move your Battalion at once to a position of readiness near Fm between BAILLEUL & FONTAINEHOUCK with Bn H.Q. at Fm.

2. You probably will have to hold a line between METEREN & Fm. Endeavour to get in touch with Units on flank, & in BAILLEUL.

3. Bde. H.Q. remains at METEREN where reports, nil or otherwise, should constantly be sent.

4. Transport and surplus remain in present camp.

5. Orders have been issued for this line to be dug by Middlesex pioneers & 222 Field Coy.

6. The enemy are reported to be holding the railway line from BAILLEUL STA to S of MERRIS.

Acknowledge.   (Sd) C. TURNER JONES Capt. RE.
                                         A/B.M. 19 Inf. Bde.

12/4/18.

2.25 p.m.

WAR DIARY.

5TH SCOTTISH RIFLES.   April, 1918.

APPENDIX No. 2.

WAR DIARY.

5TH SCOTTISH RIFLES.   April, 1918.

APPENDIX No. 1.

Copy.   B.M.638.

The Queens.
The Cameronians.
1/5 Aco. Rifles.
19th T.M.Bty.
2nd N.Z.Entrenching Bn.
18th Middlesex.
33 Div.M.G.Bn.
11th F.Coy. R.E.
22nd Corps Cyclists.

O.A. 41.
13/4/18, 11 a.m.

Following from IX Corps aaa Ninth Corps Commander wishes to congratulate all ranks on the magnificent fighting qualities which they are displaying under very arduous conditions against heavy odds aaa Reinforcements are coming up to our assistance and the enemy has suffered very heavy losses in his attempts to break through the British Armies aaa The enemy will not succeed aaa The Royal Air Force to-day crashed 47 enemy aeroplanes of which 39 were on this battle front.

Copy.

20/4/18.

My dear Spens,

I wish to take the opportunity of informing you that Captain Kirkwood and your Company did excellent work on the morning of the 17th April and were of the greatest assistance to my right Company and its Commander with whom Kirkwood was in close touch all the time. The spirit shown by them all and determination and grit with which many of them when wounded stuck to their job inspired the greatest admiration of our men and it was a great pleasure to be associated with them.

Everything quiet here since and we're wondering what the game is.

Hope everything has gone well with you and your Battalion and that later on we may meet again under similar circumstances.

With kind regards,

Yours sincerely,

(sd) B.V. STACEY.

WAR DIARY.

5TH SCOTTISH RIFLES. April, 1918.

APPENDIX No. 3.

Apps listed
1-11
missing

(C)

Army Form C. 2118.

WAR DIARY
or
INTELLIGENCE SUMMARY.
(Erase heading not required.)

5TH SCOTTISH RIFLES.

MAY, 1918.

Place	Date	Hour	Summary of Events and Information	Remarks and references to Appendices
	1		Battalion left the Aerodrome near ST MARIE CAPPEL and proceeded by march route to RACQUINGHEM where it encamped in two fields about three quarters of a mile S.W. of the village. The Battalion received a telegram of congratulation addressed by the Commander-in-Chief to the 33rd Division, see Appendix No 1.	No 1.
	2		Training carried out from 9 a.m. to 1 p.m. in the vicinity of the Camp. "A" and "B" Companies fired on the Range just north of the MELDE River and practised an attack on the way home.	
	3		Battalion proceeded by Motor Bus to the outskirts of ABEELE and then marched to some fields about two miles North of the town where it was accommodated in tents. Through this move the Battalion has now passed into the XXII Corps commanded by Lieut-General Sir A. GODLEY K.C.B. Battalion in Corps Reserve.	
	4		Battalion remained in Corps Reserve at half an hour's notice during the day. Reveille was at 5 a.m. and tents struck immediately afterwards and the camp repitched at dusk. During the afternoon as the men were unable to leave the bivouacing area a series of Boxing Matches were arranged with the 33rd Machine Gun Battalion which proved very popular. Over twenty bouts tooks place and some good boxing shown by the competitors.	
	5		Reveille at 5 a.m. The Battalion stood to arms from 7 to 7.30 a.m. Church Parade at 9.30 a.m. At 2 o'clock the Brigade moved about three quarters of a mile North of BUSSEBOOM where it was in close support to 30th Composite Brigade (attached to the 33rd Division) and 98th Brigade who were holding the line. "B" Echelon moved to field about one mile North of ABEELE.	
	6		Reconnaissances were carried out of lines in advance and also with	

Army Form C. 2118.

WAR DIARY
or
INTELLIGENCE SUMMARY.
(Erase heading not required.)

Summary of Events and Information   MAY, 1918.

Place	Date	Hour	Summary of Events and Information	Remarks and references to Appendices
	6		9th SCOTTISH RIFLES:- a view to a counter attack if required to re:capture the front system. "B" Company moved up to form a neucleus garrison in the line close to GOOD MONT MILL together with strong point near MILLE CAPELLE.	
	7		"A" Company (less one Platoon) relieved "B" Company who had had a very wet night. "C" and "D" Companies dug a support line through the night.	No. 2.
	8		The enemy delivered an attack in the early morning and drove in the 30th Composite Brigade and the right flank of the 98th Brigade. About 11 a.m. orders were received for the Battalion to move up and occupy trenches South of OUDERDOM. The Battalion moved off about 12 noon. The March up was very slow the position being reached about 3 p.m. At 3.30 p.m. orders were received (B.M.750) (Appendix No.2) for the Battalion to move round the Northern and eastern side of DICKEBUSCH LAKE and from there to deliver a counter attack along the original front line, the Battalion thus counter attacking from a flank. The Cameronians were to counter attack straight forward on the right. To get into position a march of at least four miles over ground under enemy observation had to be made and it was necessary in the first place to move the Battalion without being seen. The attack was to be delivered at 7 p.m. The Commanding Officer and Adjutant with runners pushed on to 98th Brigade Headquarters North of DICKEBUSCH selecting a route for the Battalion which would be hidden as far as possible from view as they went and sending back runners to guide the Battalion. All possible information was obtained at 98th Brigade Headquarters and the Commanding Officer and Adjutant then pushed on, after deciding on the route of march forward of the Battalion, to 2nd Argyll and Sutherland Highlanders Headquarters at the East end of the DICKEBUSCH LAKE. From there ground was studied and objectives for Companies selected. Operation order B.M.750/1 (Appendix No 3) was received and also B.M.751 (Appendix No 4) which authorised "A" Company to rejoin the Battalion. It was, however, too late to get them in time for the attack. Orders for the attack were drawn up while awaiting the arrival of the Battalion (Appendix No 5) which had to commence	No. 2. No. 4. No. 5.

Army Form C. 2118.

WAR DIARY
or
INTELLIGENCE SUMMARY.
(Erase heading not required.)

Summary of Events and Information MAY, 1918.

Place	Date	Hour	Summary of Events and Information	Remarks and references to Appendices
	8		**5TH SCOTTISH RIFLES.** commence at 3.45 when the barrage opened. The French were attacking on the right of the Cameronians at the same hour. (Appendix No 6) are also attacked. Copy of 98th Brigade Orders. The Battalion attacked with three Companies "C" "B" and "D" from left to right in Echelon. The companies assembled behind the embankments on the east of DICKEBUSCH LAKE and then advanced in echelon, one following the other, swinging round later to the left on to their objective. The first Company only reached Battalion Headquarters which were established with the 2nd Argyll & Sutherland Highlanders, from where the whole ground could be watched, at 6.30 p.m. The advance was begun at 6.45 p.m. The attack proved completely successful. A number of the enemy were killed and six machine guns and several prisoners were captured but the majority of the enemy did not wait for the attack with the bayonet. The Section leading throughout was admirable. A strong point which was holding up the advance was rushed by Sergeant Perry and three men while an enemy counter attack on the right where the flank was exposed owing to the Cameronians not having been able to gain their objectives and the 17th King's Liverpool Regiment who then attacked having not advanced as far as our own line was driven off by a determined bayonet charge led by Captain and Lieut. Kirkwood. Owing to the Cameronians being unofficially reported to have reached their objective constant efforts were made to get touch with them but no signs of them could be found. One Platoon of "A" Company which was in Battalion Reserve was sent forward about 8 p.m. to extend the line to the left where there was obviously a gap. During the night one Company 4th King's was placed at the disposal of the Battalion and were sent forward to prolong our line to the right and form a defensive flank there which was done. In /	No 6.

Army Form C. 2118.

WAR DIARY
or
INTELLIGENCE SUMMARY.

(Erase heading not required.)

Instructions regarding War Diaries and Intelligence Summaries are contained in F. S. Regs., Part II. and the Staff Manual respectively. Title pages will be prepared in manuscript.

5TH SCOTTISH RIFLES. Summary of Events and Information MAY, 1918.

Place	Date	Hour	Summary of Events and Information	Remarks and references to Appendices
	9		In the morning Aeroplane reconnaissances confirmed that the Battalion had taken all their objectives. Three Platoons of "A" Company arrived towards dawn. They were dribbled forward by sections to reinforce the line and form a support line and this operation was successfully carried out in the early morning. A Patrol to the right found no trace of the Cameronians but touch was got during the night with the 17th Kings on the right and the front line was re:organised as far as possible. The Companies were somewhat mixed but Officers were distributed along the line. Battalion Headquarters were in the morning moved to the West end of DICKEBUSCH LAKE where a joint Headquarters was established with the 17th King's who were to be relieved that night by the 1st Queens. During the 9th two Platoons 17th King's dribbled forward and filled in the gap between the right of the Battalion (Company 4th K'ng's attached) and Company of 17th King's West of VIERSTRAAT - HALLEBAST Road. On being relieved that night by the 1st Queens these two Platoons were voluntarily left by Officer Commanding 17th King's in support to our line. During the day telegram (copy attached)(Appendix No. 7) of con-gratulation was received by the Commanding Officer from the Divisional General. Things were quiet during the day except for a considerable amount of sniping which was replied to successfully. The night also passed quietly. The Queen's relieved the 17th King's on our right.	No 7
	10		In the early morning the enemy put down a heavy barrage but no Infantry action followed. A reconnoitring party of 1st Battalion 44th French Infantry Regiment came up to arrange details for relief that night. It was arranged that the Battalion, as the Relief of the Queen's would come by the same way should move out round east end of DICKEBUSCH LAKE. About 9 p.m. an S.O.S. was thought to have gone up on our front and a heavy barrage came down on both sides. It proved, however to have gone up on our right. There was no Infantry Action and the relief went on slowly, but satisfactorily. The /	

Army Form C. 2118.

WAR DIARY
or
INTELLIGENCE SUMMARY.
(Erase heading not required.)

Instructions regarding War Diaries and Intelligence Summaries are contained in F. S. Regs., Part II. and the Staff Manual respectively. Title pages will be prepared in manuscript.

Place	Date	Hour	Summary of Events and Information	Remarks and references to Appendices
5TH SCOTTISH RIFLES.			MAY, 1918.	
	11		The French were attacking at dawn. The relief was completed about 3.45 a.m. The Battalion moved back to bivouacs N.W. of BUSSEBOOM. Later in the day the Battalion moved to a camp near DIRTY BUCKET CORNER. The Minimum Reserve and "B" Echelon moved their camp to a field about 1,000 yards S.E. of St JAN-TER-BIEZEN.	
	12		Minimum Reserve and "B" Echelon re:joined the Battalion at the hutment camps at DIRTY BUCKET during the forenoon by march route. The Battalion was inspected in the afternoon along with the first Cameronians by the XXII Corps Commander, Lieut-General Sir A.J. GODLEY, K.C.B., K.C.M.G., and addressed by him afterwards and congratulated on its good work during the recent operations. The Divisional General also addressed the troops. After the Inspection parade a short Church Parade was held for both Battalions which was attended by the Brigadier. Copies of the Divisional General and Corps Commander's speeches are attached (Appendix No. 8)	No 8
	13		Training was carried out under Company arrangements during the morning and the reorganisation of platoons and Sections completed.	
	14		Musketry, Physical Training, Bayonet Fighting and Close Order Drill carried out by Companies from 9.15 a.m. to 12.30 p.m. Classes for N.C.Os held during the afternoon. A Battalion concert was held in the Church Army Hut at 6 p.m.	
	15		The Commanding Officer inspected every platoon in the Battalion starting with "C" Company at 9.15 a.m. After being inspected each platoon carried on with Drill, Musketry, Physical Training and Bayonet Fighting until 12.30 p.m. Classes for N.C.Os were held in the afternoon from 2 to 3.30 by the R.S.M. and C.Sgt. Majors.	
	16		"A" Company paraded at 8 a.m. and marched to a point 2,000 yards	

S.W./

WAR DIARY
or
INTELLIGENCE SUMMARY.
(Erase heading not required.)

Army Form C. 2118.

5TH SCOTTISH RIFLES.   Summary of Events and Information   MAY, 1918.

Place	Date	Hour	Summary of Events and Information	Remarks and references to Appendices
	16		S.W. of POPERINGHE on the main POPERINGHE - STEENVOORDE Road where it embussed for RUBROUCK to carry out a two days' musketry programme there. The rest of the Battalion carried out training during the morning and afternoon in extraordinarily hot weather.	
	17		Usual training carried out in very hot weather. "A" Company at RUBROUCK.	
	18		The Battalion moved with the rest of the Brigade back to the ABEELE area very early in the morning and was located in tents about 3,000 yards N. of ABEELE. "A" Company from RUBROUCK rejoined Battalion at night having been brought by Motor Busses.	
	19		Church parades held during the morning for the various denominations. The Commanding Officer inspected the Camp at 11.45 a.m. A Draft of 36 Other Ranks arrived from the Base.	
	20		Commanding Officer's parade at 7 a.m. when movements to be done at the Army Commander's Inspection today were rehearsed. The Brigadier inspected the Regimental Transport. At 11 o'clock the Battalion paraded with the rest of the 19th Infantry Brigade for Inspection by the Second Army Commander, General SIR HERBERT C.O.PLUMER, G.C.B., G.C.M.G., G.C.V.O., A.D.C., at mid-day. The Army Commander walked round the ranks of the Brigade after which he presented Military Medals to N.C.Os and men of the 33rd Division won during the recent METEREN fighting and then addressed the Brigade. The proceedings concluded with a march past in column of fours.	
	21		Battalion paraded for Physical Training and Games at 7 a.m. Training carried out from 9 a.m. to 12 noon and Specialist training during the afternoon. Instruction of N.C.Os during the evening. AT /	

Army Form C. 2118.

WAR DIARY
or
INTELLIGENCE SUMMARY.
(Erase heading not required.)

Instructions regarding War Diaries and Intelligence Summaries are contained in F. S. Regs., Part II. and the Staff Manual respectively. Title pages will be prepared in manuscript.

Place	Date	Hour	Summary of Events and Information	Remarks and references to Appendices
5TH SCOTTISH RIFLES.			MAY, 1918.	
	21		At 2 p.m. the Commanding Officer presented the cards sent by General Pinney Commanding the 33rd Division to Officers and men of the Battalion who distinguished themselves in the Field during the operations from 8th to 11th May inclusive.	
	22		Early morning parade from 7.20 to 7.50 for Physical Training and Games. Forenoon parade 9.20 to 11.30 a.m. Each Company spent one hour at the 30 yards range during the day and one hour at the GAS HUT passing through lachrymatory gas. Specialist Training was carried out during the evening and N.C.Os classes held at the same time.	
	23		Training programme carried out similar to the previous day. The Divisional General rode round the Battalion during the early morning parade. The whole Battalion proceeded to the Baths during the day.	
	24		Reveille at 2.15 a.m. and the Battalion paraded at 4 a.m. and marched up to huts near BUSSEBOOM relieving the 2nd Worcesters as one of the Battalions of the Advanced Brigade of Second Corps reserve. Very wet day. The VLAMERTINGHE and BRANDHOEK lines were reconnoitred during the afternoon.	
	25		"A", "B" and "C" Companies paraded at 4 a.m. and marched to DIRTY BUCKET CAMP where they met guides and worked under the R.Es. on the BRANDHOEK Line and the BRANDHOEK Support Line returning to their huts at 11 a.m. "D" Company proceeded by motor busses to RUBROUCK for three days musketry.	
	26		BUCKET CAMP and again worked on the BRANDHOEK line. "A", "B" and "C" Companies paraded at 4 a.m. and marched to DIRTY Voluntary /	

Army Form C. 2118.

WAR DIARY
or
INTELLIGENCE SUMMARY.
(Erase heading not required.)

Instructions regarding War Diaries and Intelligence Summaries are contained in F.S. Regs., Part II. and the Staff Manual respectively. Title pages will be prepared in manuscript.

Place	Date	Hour	Summary of Events and Information	Remarks and references to Appendices
5TH SCOTTISH RIFLES.			MAY, 1918.	
	26		Voluntary Church Parades during the afternoon. "D" Company at RUBROUCK.	
	27		"A", "B" and "C" companies carried out training from 7 to 10 a.m. The Commanding Officer visited "D" Company at RUBROUCK.	
	28	11 a.m.	"A", "B" and "C" Companies carried out training from 8 a.m. until "D" Company returned from RUBROUCK. Some shelling of the area in which the Battalion is located and three men wounded.	
	29	9.30 a.m.	"B" and "C" Companies worked on the BRANDHOEK line from 5 to "D" Company worked on the POPERINGHE East Line during the same hours. The List of honours and awards gained by the Battalion during the recent fighting received (Appendix No 9)	No 9
	30	to 9.30 a.m.	"A", "B" and "C" Companies worked on the BRANDHOEK line from 5 "D" Company worked on the POPERINGHE East Line during the same hours.	
	31		Training carried out during the morning under Company arrangements. Copy of GENERAL PINNEY'S speech given at the Aerodrome near ST MARIE CAPPEL at the end of last month attached (in Appendix 10.) also lists of honours and awards for last month's operations. (Appendix No 10 a) Copy of the Lord Provost of Glasgow's Letter received by Lieut-Col. H.B.SPENS, D.S.O. attached (Appendix 11.)	No 10 No 10 a No. 11.
			Casualties /	

Army Form C. 2118.

WAR DIARY
or
INTELLIGENCE SUMMARY.
(Erase heading not required.)

Place	Date	Hour	Summary of Events and Information	Remarks and references to Appendices
5TH SCOTTISH RIFLES.			MAY, 1918.	
			CASUALTIES.	
			OFFICERS.	
			2nd Lieut. J.R. GRANT killed in action 8/5/18.	
			do. W. CRAIG, do. do.	
			Lieut. M. BLAIR wounded 8/5/18.	
			2nd Lieut. R.S.L.FORRET,M.C. wounded 8/5/18 since died of wounds.	
			Captain J.KIRKWOOD wounded, at duty 8/5/18 To Hospital 13/5/18.	
			2nd Lieut. R. DAVIE wounded at duty 8/5/18.	
			do. W.McC.SMITH do. do.	
			do. T.C. CUTHBERTSON wounded (Gas) 9/5/18.	
			OTHER RANKS.	
			Killed 33 Wounded 179 Missing 16.	
			Reinforcements received during the month.	
			Officers. Other Ranks.	
			Capt. A.D. Hart	
			" A.C. Stewart.	
			" T. Shearer. 155.	
			Lieut. N.P. Paxton.	
			2/Lieut. D.McL. Baird.	
			" A.B. McRae. M.C.	
			" A. Paterson.	
			" A. Anderson.	
			" A. Baird.	
			" J.P. Clark.	
			Strength of Battalion.	
			Officers. 40. Other Ranks 785.	
			Cmdg. 5th Scottish Rifles. Lieut.-Col.,	

Army Form C. 2118.

Vol 44

WAR DIARY
or
INTELLIGENCE SUMMARY.
(Erase heading not required.)

Place	Date	Hour	Summary of Events and Information	Remarks and references to Appendices
5th Scottish Rifles	2nd		Battalion was relieved at OXLEY FARM by 1st Middlesex Regt. and moved back to HUSBAND CAMP, ROOSENDAAL vacated by the 2nd Argyll and Sutherland Highlanders.	45-0 4 sheets
	3rd/5th		Usual training carried out.	
	6th		The Battalion attended Baths in the forenoon. The Annual Sports were held in the afternoon & evening.	
	7th		The Battalion entrained at REMY SOUTH, detrained at Machine Gun Farm and relieved the 1st Kings Shropshire Light Infantry in the Left Front Brigade Sector, two Companies "A" and "B" occupying the front line of posts with "C" Coy in Support in the G.H.Q. No 1 Line and "D" Company in Reserve. During this tour in the line a few American Officers and N.C.Os were attached for instructional purposes.	
	13th		The Battalion (less "C" Coy) was relieved by the 1st Queens (less one Company) in the front line of posts and in reserve	

WAR DIARY
or
INTELLIGENCE SUMMARY.

Army Form C. 2118.

Place	Date	Hour	Summary of Events and Information	Remarks and references to Appendices
5th Scottish Rifles			June, 1918.	
			"A" Company moved to G.H.Q. No 1 Line beside "C" Company and both came under the orders of the Officer Commanding 1st Queens for tactical purposes. "B" and "D" Companies took over Bivouacs and Dugouts vacated by the 1st Queens in Brigade Reserve positions near the BROWN LINE and BELGIAN CHATEAU.	
	14th		Working parties were supplied by B and D Coys for work on BROWN LINE under the REs.	
	15th		The Battalion was relieved in the Brown Line and G.H.Q No 1 Line by the 9th Highland Light Infantry taking up positions in the YELLOW and GREEN LINES with Battalion Head-quarters at ERIE CAMP, BRANDHOEK.	
	16/19th		Working parties were supplied to REs and 18th Middlesex Pioneers for improvements &c on GREEN LINE and at QUERY FARM.	
	20th			

Army Form C. 2118.

WAR DIARY
or
INTELLIGENCE SUMMARY.
(Erase heading not required.)

Instructions regarding War Diaries and Intelligence Summaries are contained in F. S. Regs., Part II. and the Staff Manual respectively. Title pages will be prepared in manuscript.

Place	Date	Hour	Summary of Events and Information	Remarks and references to Appendices
5th Scottish Rifles			June 1918.	
	20th		The Battalion relieved the 2nd Argyle & Sutherland High- landers in the Right Front Right Sub Sector of the Canal Sector.	
	20th/30th		During this tour in the lines liaison was had with the French (Chasseurs) on the right and American Officers and N.C.Os were attached to the Battalion for experience in Trench warfare. Messenger dogs were employed between front Companies and Battalion Headquarters.	
	30th		The Battalion was relieved by the 3rd Worcestershire Regt. and took up positions vacated by that Regiment near the YELLOW and GREEN LINES with Headquarters at KNOLLYS FARM.	
BRANDHOEK			Reinforcements received during month :-	
			2nd Lieut Baird A. ⎫ Lieut Millar C.J. ⎫ Other Ranks Smith J.H. ⎬ 2/Lt Ford D.W. ⎬ 179 " Shearer Y.M.C. ⎭ Capt White M.M.K. ⎭ 7 Officers	
			Capt Robertson Smith A.M.	

WAR DIARY
or
INTELLIGENCE SUMMARY.

Army Form C. 2118.

5th Scottish Rifles   June 1918.

Casualties

———— Officers ————   ———— Other Ranks ————

2/Lieut. Kerr A.G. wounded   Killed   3
(1 p.m. 29/6/18.)   Died of Wounds 1
                                Wounded   30
                                Missing   1
                                               ___
                                               35

———— Padres ————

Capt. R. Stowe joined to U.S. 25/6/18.
"   S.O. Stewart joined   28/6/18.

———— Battalion Strength ————

43 Officers.   864 other Ranks.

Officers to/H
5th Scottish Rifles
O.Mag 5th Scottish Rifles

Army Form C. 2118.
5 Scottish Rifles

WAR DIARY
or
INTELLIGENCE SUMMARY.
(Erase heading not required.)

Instructions regarding War Diaries and Intelligence Summaries are contained in F. S. Regs., Part II. and the Staff Manual respectively. Title pages will be prepared in manuscript.

5TH SCOTTISH RIFLES   Summary of Events and Information   JULY, 1918.

Place	Date	Hour	Summary of Events and Information	Remarks and references to Appendices
Brandhoek.	1st		Battalion in Divisional Reserve with Headquarters KNOLLY'S FARM. The day was allotted to the Battalion for bathing and all Companies were bathed at VLAMERTINGHE.	
	2nd		All Companies worked on GREEN LINE in the forenoon and "A" and "C" Companies were out at night carrying Ammunition etc to establish a dump close by Battalion Headquarters.	
	3rd		The Battalion was again allotted the day for bathing, this time at TORONTO CAMP. Nothing of importance happened during the remainder of the day.	
	4th		Companies were again working on the GREEN LINE during the forenoon. Hostile shelling was a bit more active to-day and one shell landed beside "B" Company wounding 7 men.	
	5th		"D" Company went to VIJERBEKE, "B" Company to BELGIAN CHATEAU and "C" Company in trenches round about Battalion Headquarters. "A" Company took over a Company front from the 9th H.L.I. in the G.H.Q.No 2 Line Right Sub-Sector and were under the command of THE CAMERONIANS for 24 hours. The Battalion relieved the 1st MIDDLESEX REGIMENT (98th Brigade) the relief being very good and completed by 12 midnight.	
	6th		Very quiet day. "A" Company were relieved from G.H.Q.No 2 Line by a Company of THE CAMERONIANS and came back to BROWN LINE beside "C" Company round about Battalion Headquarters. Good relief and completed by 11 p.m.	

Army Form C. 2118.

WAR DIARY
or
INTELLIGENCE SUMMARY.
(Erase heading not required.)

Instructions regarding War Diaries and Intelligence Summaries are contained in F. S. Regs., Part II. and the Staff Manual respectively. Title pages will be prepared in manuscript.

Place	Date	Hour	Summary of Events and Information	Remarks and references to Appendices
5TH SCOTTISH RIFLES.			JULY, 1918.	
	7th		"B" Company supplied a working party of two Officers and 50 Other Ranks to work on G.H.Q. No 3 Line with THE QUEEN'S. "C" and "D" Companies also supplied working parties for work under the R.Es.	
	8th		Working parties were again supplied by all Companies as on the previous day. THE QUEEN'S (who had to send a large party to take part in the 14th July celebrations at PARIS) were withdrawn from the front line and this Battalion relieved them. Capt. J.KIRKWOOD, M.C., took over command of THE QUEEN'S. The relief which was very quiet took a bit longer than usual and was not reported complete till about 3 a.m. on the 9th. "A" Company RIGHT FRONT COY. "B" " LEFT FRONT COY. "C" " SUPPORT. "D" " RESERVE. "C" Company went into the front line on the night of the 8th but were relieved on the 9th by "B" Company and came back to support.	
	9th		Quiet day on the whole with very little Artillery or E.A. activity. At night an inter-company relief took place between "B" and "C" Companies, "B" Company going into the Front Line (LEFT FRONT) and "C" Company coming back to SUPPORT. Capt J. KIRKWOOD, M.C., returned to the Battalion. Lieut. W.R.PAXTON took out a patrol at night and after patrolling 'No-man's Land' for some time was challenged from a German post at I 27 c 60.55. The enemy receiving no reply fired and threw bombs at our patrol. No casualties were caused and patrol returned to our lines.	
	10th		A wet day. Lieut PAXTON and 2/Lieut R. DAVIE with 15 Other Ranks went out to reconnoitre the suspected post at I 27 c 60.55. The patrol separated	

Army Form C. 2118.

WAR DIARY
or
INTELLIGENCE SUMMARY.
(Erase heading not required.)

Instructions regarding War Diaries and Intelligence Summaries are contained in F. S. Regs., Part II. and the Staff Manual respectively. Title pages will be prepared in manuscript.

Place	Date	Hour	Summary of Events and Information	Remarks and references to Appendices
			5TH SCOTTISH RIFLES. JULY, 1918.	
	10th		into two parties each under an Officer. The two parties moved cautiously over the ground till within fifteen yards of the suspected post. At this point Lieut. DAVIE who was on the right discovered an unoccupied enemy bombing post with a supply of egg bombs in it. Lieut Davie and Lce./Cpl. Turnbull started to enter the post and when doing so a can was rattled this being a signal to the Bosch in the farm building at I 27 c 60.55 who immediately opened fire and threw bombs at our patrol. Lieut Davie had four men wounded but all were brought back safely to our lines.	
	11th		Quiet day. Four new Officers joined the Battalion, three remaining at the Transport Lines and one (Lieut. A. HAMILTON) came up to Battalion Headquarters to take over the duties of Signalling Officer.	
	12th		Very quiet day. Arrangements made with Artillery, T.M. and M.G. for co-operation in raid to take place night 13th/14th.	
	13th		The Commanding Officer attended a Conference at Brigade Headquarters where the final details for the raid were completed. The raiding party commanded by Capt. R.W.BEGG assembled at BEDFORD HOUSE and moved off from there in three parties. "A" Company's party under 2/Lieut. A.G.KERR and Lieut.D.M.BAIRD "C" Company's party under Lieut. A.B.MCCRAE and 2/Lieut. A.PATERSON. The third party composed of two Lewis Gun Teams from "D" Company was under C.S.M. Stevenson. The Party took up a position 150 yards behind the objective, 15 minutes before ZERO, the ZERo hour being 12.25 a.m. 14th. During the Artillery, T.M. and M.G. bombardment the raiding party went forward as near as possible to the objective and at ZERO plus 5 minutes they rushed the post. The Germans were not there, however, and after searching dug-outs etc the raiding party returned to our lines. The party sustained 10 casualties i.e. 1 killed, 7 wounded and Lieut.A.PATERSON and one other rank missing.	

Army Form C. 2118.

WAR DIARY
or
INTELLIGENCE SUMMARY.
(Erase heading not required.)

5TH SCOTTISH RIFLES. Summary of Events and Information JULY, 1918.

Place	Date	Hour	Summary of Events and Information	Remarks and references to Appendices
	14th		Very quiet day with nothing of importance to record.	
	15th		Today completes the tour of the Battalion in the line and at night it was relieved by the 2nd WORCESTERSHIRE REGIMENT. Very little shelling during the day but E.A. was fairly active. The relief commenced about 4.45 p.m. and was a very good one all Companies reporting complete by 12.30 a.m. 16th. The Germans shelled the road and Light Railway at BELGIAN BATTERY CORNER as the companies were proceeding past there and "B" Company had one man killed and one wounded. The Battalion moved back to Divisional Reserve, Battn. Headquarters being at KNOLLY'S FARM.	
	16th		The Baths at VLAMERTINGHE were at the disposal of the Battalion today and all the men had a Bath and clean change of clothing. The day was quiet. Major Scott, M.C. arrived from Minimum Reserve and assumed command of the Battalion.	
	17th		Working parties were supplied by "B", "C" and "D" Companies in the forenoon. Intelligence Officer visited the 2nd Argyll and Sutherland Highlanders and made arrangements for relief to be carried out on the night of 20th/21st inst.	
	18th		Very quiet day with nothing of importance to report.	
	19th		Another quiet day with very little hostile shelling or E.A. activity. A test was carried out in the afternoon between the R.A.F. and Infantry. An aeroplane came over the GREEN LINE at 3.15 p.m. and called for flares by means of the Klaxton Horn. Our men in the trenches displayed discs to the aeroplane who apparently noticed them alright and indicated so by sending R.D. on the Klaxton Horn. A similar practice was carried out at	

Army Form C. 2118.

WAR DIARY
or
INTELLIGENCE SUMMARY.

(Erase heading not required.)

5TH SCOTTISH RIFLES. Summary of Events and Information **JULY, 1918.**

Date	Hour	Summary of Events and Information
19th		Battalion Headquarters but this time it was sending messages by means of the T panel. The Aeroplane hovered over-head and our Signallers sent up messages, the Observer sending R.D. on the Klaxton when he had received the message. The stunt was carried out very quickly and from all appearances seemed to be a success.
20th		Quiet during the day. At night the Battalion relieved the 2nd Argyll & Sutherland Highlanders who were holding the Left Battalion Front, Sub-Sector CANAL sector. The relief was very quiet and speedily got through, all Companies reporting Relief complete by 11.25 p.m. "D" Company Right Front Company. "C" " Left do. "A" " Right Support. "B" " Left Support. We took over two Companies of the 1/119th American Infantry Regiment from the 2nd Argyll and Sutherland Highlanders. Half Company Americans attached to each of our Companies for instruction.
21st		Fairly quiet day but at night counter preparations were carried out by the Artillery it being rumoured that the enemy would attack early on the morning of 22nd. Nothing happened however. A good many casualties were sustained during the night by the Battalion.
22nd		The Americans take over the Battalion front from us to-night for 48 hours. They relieve our four Companies by three of theirs and we withdraw to the Green line for the time being. The Commanding Officer (Major Scott, M.C.) and Lieut A. Hamilton,(Signalling Officer)with a proportion of N.C.Os and Signallers remained in the line with the American Troops. The relief was quite a good one but took a bit longer than usual owing to the Artillery carrying out counter preparation bursts and our troops had to take cover for a bit. Relief was reported complete about 3 a.m.

Army Form C. 2118.

WAR DIARY
or
INTELLIGENCE SUMMARY.
(Erase heading not required.)

5TH SCOTTISH RIFLES.   Summary of Events and Information   **JULY 1918.**

Place	Date	Hour	Summary of Events and Information	Remarks and references to Appendices
	23rd		Very quiet day on the whole both Artillery and E.A. being very inactive.	
	24th		Intelligence Officer went up to 2/119th American Infantry Regiment fixing up details with them about their going into the line with the Battalion at night. Two Companies of Americans came up at 6.30 a.m. and joined our Battalion in the Green line remaining there all day until dusk when they go forward with us to the Front Line. Relief commenced from Green Line at 8.30 p.m. and it was a very quiet and speedy one. All Companies reported relief complete by 11.30 p.m. Only 12 men per platoon (British) were sent into the line the remainder being left behind in the Green Line under command of Capt. M.M. Robertson Smith, and Lieut. S.L.Brand Crombie. Captain Hobbs and Battalion Staff of the 2/119th Battalion U.S.A. Infantry came into the line and were attached to the Headquarters of the Battalion.	
	25th		Slight shelling of the whole area occupied by the Battalion. Tartan Patches arrived for the Battalion and the Tailors started to sew them on the shoulders of the men's coats.	
	26th		Battalion heavily shelled all day causing a good many casualties. Very wet night.	
	27th		Battalion front and support areas were shelled actively throughout the day with all calibres up to 8" including a few blue cross gas. We suffered no casualties. The night was quiet.	
	28th		Except for slight spasmodic hostile shelling the enemy maintained an inoffensive attitude on the front. Relief of 51st Landwehr Division opposite our Divisional Sector is suspected.	
	29th		Hostile activity on our front and support areas between 10 p.m. and 12 midnight with slight harassing fire which had no results. Hostile aerial	

Army Form C. 2118.

WAR DIARY
or
INTELLIGENCE SUMMARY.

(Erase heading not required.)

Instructions regarding War Diaries and Intelligence Summaries are contained in F. S. Regs., Part II. and the Staff Manual respectively. Title pages will be prepared in manuscript.

Place	Date	Hour	Summary of Events and Information	Remarks and references to Appendices
5TH SCOTTISH RIFLES.			JULY, 1918.	
	29th		Poor visibility throughout the day. reconnaissance attempted before dusk. During the night E. & G. Companies of 2nd Battalion 119th U.S. Infantry Regiment took over the front line (Left Battalion) and our forward Companies withdrew to the Support positions, A and D under Capt. A.C. Stewart being on the Right and B. and C under Capt. C.E.Grant on the left. Capt. J.Kirkwood and Capt. A.D.Hart with their Headquarter Details remained at Right and Left Company Headquarters respectively with the American Companies. All relief's had been completed by 2.45 a.m.(30/7/18) Advance parties of 1 Officer per Company and 1 N.C.O. per Platoon from 9th H.L.I. proceeded about 10 p.m. to respective Company Sub-Sectors to be taken over by latter Battalion on night of 1st/2nd August.	
	30th		Nothing of unusual interest occurred during the day. Shortly after 9.30 p.m. movement started for relief of the Battalion by "F" and "H" Companies of the 2nd Battalion 119th American Infantry Regiment in Support Trenches Left Battalion Sub-Sector (Right Sector, Canal Sector.) Relief was carried out without incident and reported complete by 11.45 p.m. Battalion proceeded to BRANDHOEK Support Line - Battalion Headquarters at Sheet 28 G. 11 d 3.2. Thick haze during the night 30th/31st July. Weather warm and dry.	
	31st.		Battalion resting and cleaning up.	

Army Form C. 2118.

WAR DIARY
or
INTELLIGENCE SUMMARY.
(Erase heading not required.)

5TH SCOTTISH RIFLES Summary of Events and Information JULY 1918.

CASUALTIES DURING MONTH.

Officers.	Other Ranks.

2/Lt. A. Paterson missing 15/7/18.   Killed   5.
 "   J.H. Smith killed 25/7/18.   Wounded   49.
 "   A.H. Frame wounded do.   Missing.   2.

REINFORCEMENTS RECEIVED DURING MONTH.

Lieut. G. Fraser.
  "   A. Hamilton.   Other Ranks 115.
2/Lt. A.G. Kerr.
  "   A.H. Frame.
  "   J.H. Smith.

STRENGTH.

Officers. 42.   Other Ranks. 880.

AlexRSpr. Lieut-Col.,
Cmdg. 5th Scottish Rifles.

WAR DIARY
or
INTELLIGENCE SUMMARY.
(Erase heading not required.)

Army Form C. 2118.

5 Scottish Rifles

Place	Date	Hour	Summary of Events and Information	Remarks and references to Appendices
5TH SCOTTISH RIFLES.			AUGUST, 1918.	
	1	6.30 a.m.	A Demonstration was carried out by "D" Company in the area (Sheet 28 H 1d.) and attended by Officers and N.C.Os. of the other three Companies. It showed the advance behind creeping barrage (represented by Signallers with flags), the deployment of Platoons attacking and enveloping a strong point &c. The Battalion had the use of the baths near TORONTO CAMP for the day, and a clean change of underclothing and socks was issued there. Scouts' Class in the open was taken by two platoons in the evening. A. and B. Companies each supplied two platoons as nucleus Garrison in GREEN LINE (Right sector), when 9th Highland Light Infantry moved thence into Front Line system.	
	2		Party of 4 Officers and 46 Other Ranks under Capt. J. KIRKWOOD, M.C., embussed at Brigade Headquarters at 5.45 a.m. and proceeded to ST MALO near DUNKIRK where they spent the day, returning from there at 5 p.m. Working parties comprising 250 Other Ranks were supplied for 4 hours work (7/11 a.m.) in the GREEN LINE (Sheet 28/ H 8 d and 13 d). Remainder of C and D Companies carried out training during the morning in vicinity of their huts. Rifles and Lewis Guns in the Battalion were inspected by the Armourer Sergeant.	
	3		Working parties 250 strong on GREEN and YELLOW LINES during forenoon. Barr and Stroud Range Finders adjusted by Armourer Sergeant. Adjutant visited Headquarters of 2nd Battalion Argyll & Sutherland Highlanders (Support Left Canal Sector) and arranged details of relief for following day.	
	4		Advance party from 2nd A. & S.H. took over our dispositions in YELLOW LINE (Right Sector). Battalion relieved 2nd A. & S.H. in Support (Left Brigade Sector) without incident.	

WAR DIARY
or
INTELLIGENCE SUMMARY.
(Erase heading not required.)

Army Form C. 2118.

Place	Date	Hour	Summary of Events and Information	Remarks and references to Appendices
5TH SCOTTISH RIFLES.			AUGUST, 1918.	
	5		Quiet day. Working parties (which will continue during the tour) were detailed from company and engaged in improving the defences in left Sector under supervision of R.Es.	
	6		An ordinary day with nothing of importance to record in the forward area. General PLUMER inspected Minimum Reserve and expressed his satisfaction. Officers and men of Minimum Reserve went to LA LOVIE CHATEAU and lined avenue on departure of the KING.	
	7		Another uneventful day: the usual Routine.	
	8		No special activity on the front.	
	9		Pronounced Aerial Activity on our part during the day. Enemy submissive.	
	10		Nothing of particular interest occurred beyond the usual Routine.	
	11		Party from Minimum Reserve represented the Battalion in the March Past after the Special Service at TERDEGHEM attended by HIS MAJESTY the KING. Weather warm and hazy.	
	12		Normal day. Companies busy on trench repairs and Working parties according to programme.	
	13		All Companies carried out training with Bombs and Rifle Grenades in the Support Area. After dusk B Company evacuated and occupied posts in the intermediate line (left Sector) with Company Headquarters in BELGIAN CHATEAU.	
	14		Battalion relieved by 2nd WORCESTER REGIMENT in Support (Left Sector) and proceeded to YELLOW LINE (Left Sub-Sector) with Battalion Headquarters	

Army Form C. 2118.

WAR DIARY
or
INTELLIGENCE SUMMARY.
(Erase heading not required.)

Instructions regarding War Diaries and Intelligence Summaries are contained in F. S. Regs., Part II. and the Staff Manual respectively. Title pages will be prepared in manuscript.

5TH SCOTTISH RIFLES.   Summary of Events and Information   AUGUST, 1918.

Place	Date	Hour	Summary of Events and Information	Remarks and references to Appendices
at ERIE FARM.	15		Relief completed by 11.50 p.m. Casualties NIL. Following is copy of letter from 33rd Division to 19th Infantry Brigade and passed to the Battalion on 6/8/18 :- "It has been brought to notice of the Divisional Commander that very good work has been carried out by the 5th Battalion Scottish Rifles on the YELLOW LINE during the past few days. He would be glad if you would convey his appreciation to all ranks of the Battalion." On the night of the 15th/16th August, 1918 the Battalion was relieved in the left sub-sector YELLOW LINE by the 2nd 119th Regiment (AMERICAN) and after relief marched via ST JAN TER BEIZEN to GABB and CHASE CAMPS.	
	16		Day was at the disposal of Company Commanders and was given to cleaning up and kit inspections.	
	17		Battalion carried out training in fields in the vicinity of the Camp during the forenoon. "A" Company was inspected by the Brigadier General and afterwards by the Commanding Officer.	
	18		A DRUM HEAD SERVICE in the 1st Cameronians' Camp at 11.30 a.m. was attended by both Battalions and conducted by Captain S.O.STEWART, C.F. The Band of the 119th American Regiment was present. Advance party proceeded to EPERLECQUES Area on billetting duty also second line Transport started for this destination by Road.	
	19		At 10.30 a.m. the battalion left GABB and CHASE CAMPS and marched to PROVEN STATION where it entrained. First Line Transport followed by train 2 hours later as far as ST OMER, thence Road to BAYENGHEM. personnel detrained at WATTEN STATION and marched to Billets in BAYENGHEM - LES - EPERLECQUES.	

Army Form C. 2118.

WAR DIARY
or
INTELLIGENCE SUMMARY.
(Erase heading not required.)

Instructions regarding War Diaries and Intelligence Summaries are contained in F. S. Regs., Part II. and the Staff Manual respectively. Title pages will be prepared in manuscript.

5TH SCOTTISH RIFLES.   Summary of Events and Information   AUGUST, 1918.

Place	Date	Hour	Summary of Events and Information	Remarks and references to Appendices
	20		The Battalion and all Transport started from BAYENGHEM at 9.30 a.m. by road to LICQUES Area arriving about 3 p.m. Headquarters and A Company near HOCQUINGHEM and B, C and D Companies near HERBINGHEM. Battalion Headquarters and details were billeted in the Chateau and the Companies in Farms in the Area.	
	21		Inspections and Training were carried out during the forenoon under Company arrangements. A lecture on Training was given by the Commanding Officer to all Officers and N.C.Os. in the afternoon.	
	22		The forenoon and part of the afternoon was devoted to training of 11 Platoons, Signallers and Scouts under their own Officers in suitable areas near HERBINGHEM. Special performance was given by the Regimental Pipe Band in the evening in the grounds of CHATEAU DU ROUGEFORT (South of LICQUES.)	
	23	9 PM	Training was continued as on the previous day. Billets were taken over for the Battalion in another area and the following were the new dispositions:— Battalion Headquarters and Details AUDENFORT A Company LE POIRIER B, C and D Companies AUDREHEM.	
	24		Battalion on training. In the evening the "SHRAPNELS" Divisional Concert Party performed in the grounds of AUDREHEM CHATEAU.	
	25		Church Parade at AUDREHEM. Party of 1 Officer and 25 Other Ranks from the Battalion were allowed to ST MALO for the day travelling by Motor Lorry. Capt. H.W.BARBER, R.A.M.C. joined the Battalion and took over duties of Medical Officer from Lieut. A.L.JONES M.C., M.O.R.C., U.S.R. who proceeded the following day under instructions to report to O.C. American Army Laboratory, DIJON.	

Army Form C. 2118.

WAR DIARY
or
INTELLIGENCE SUMMARY.
(Erase heading not required.)

Instructions regarding War Diaries and Intelligence Summaries are contained in F. S. Regs., Part II. and the Staff Manual respectively. Title pages will be prepared in manuscript.

5TH SCOTTISH RIFLES.   Summary of Events and Information   AUGUST, 1918.

Place	Date	Hour	Summary of Events and Information	Remarks and references to Appendices
	26		The Division received orders for transfer from 2nd Army to 3rd Army. 19th Infantry Brigade group marched to LUMBRES Area and the Battalion rested for the night in Camp at SAMETTE.	
	27		Entraining Orders received. 3 Officers from the Battalion proceeded by car to FREVENT to remain at Station there on detraining duty for all units of the Brigade under Capt F.O.THORNE, M.C. Manchester Regiment. Advanced billeting party of 1 Officer and Interpreter proceeded by Lorry from Brigade Headquarters to BOU QUEMAISON thence to LE SOUICH. One Company ("A") plus Cooker to moved to WIZERNES and entrained there at 1 a.m. 28/8/18. On arrival at FREVENT this Company was accommodated in the Rest Camp and supplied unloading parties during the detrainment of Brigade Group. At 10.30 p.m. Battalion Transport and at 12 midnight B,C and D Companies and Headquarter Details left SAMETTE and marched to entraining station at WIZERNES.	
	28		About 10.30 a.m. the Battalion (less ACompany) arrived at FREVENT Tea was provided free at Station by Divisional Canteen and thereafter the Battalion (less "A"Company) plus Transport marched to billets in LE SOUICH (Somme).	
	29		Companies at disposal of Company Commanders for cleaning up, light training etc. "A" Company rejoined Battalion from FREVENT.	
	30		All Units of the 19th Infantry Brigade paraded on the open ground immediately North East of LE SOUICH at 10.30 a.m. and awaited the arrival of the Divisional Commander (General Sir R.PINNEY,K.C.B) who inspected the Brigade, presented Medal Ribands to Officers and other ranks and afterwards witnessed a March Past. General PINNEY'S short address to the Troops was appreciative and confident. The afternoon was free for games.	

Army Form C. 2118.

WAR DIARY
or
INTELLIGENCE SUMMARY.

(Erase heading not required.)

Instructions regarding War Diaries and Intelligence Summaries are contained in F. S. Regs., Part II. and the Staff Manual respectively. Title pages will be prepared in manuscript.

Place	Date	Hour	Summary of Events and Information	Remarks and references to Appendices
5TH SCOTTISH RIFLES.			AUGUST, 1918.	
	31		scheme of attack in the open South West of IVERGNY. In the afternoon a Lecture by the Commanding Officer on "THE ATTACK" (in open warfare) was attended by all Officers and N.C.O. Platoon Commanders of this Battalion.	
			Reinforcements received during month :-	
			OFFICERS. OTHER RANKS.	
			Lieut. N. CLARK, M.M.	
			" R. DOWNIE, D.C.M.	
			" G. GUNN. 41	
			2/Lt. W. OG.PATTISON	
			" J. YOUNG.	
			Casualties during month :-	
			NIL. Wounded 5. T	
			Wounded at duty. 2.	
			Strength of Battalion:-	
			Officers. 45	
			Other Ranks. 901.	

[signature]
Lieut.-Col.
Commanding 5th Scottish Rifles.

Army Form C. 2118.

WAR DIARY
or
INTELLIGENCE SUMMARY.
(Erase heading not required.)

Instructions regarding War Diaries and Intelligence Summaries are contained in F. S. Regs., Part II. and the Staff Manual respectively. Title pages will be prepared in manuscript.

Place	Date	Hour	Summary of Events and Information	Remarks and references to Appendices
			Casualties during the month — NIL	
			Strength of Battalion	
			OFFICERS — 39	
			OTHER RANKS — 918	
			[signature] LIEUT COL. COMMANDING 5TH SCOTTISH RIFLES	

Army Form C. 2118.

WAR DIARY
or
INTELLIGENCE SUMMARY.
(Erase heading not required.)

5TH SCOTTISH RIFLES.   Summary of Events and Information   SEPTEMBER, 1918.

Place	Date	Hour	Summary of Events and Information	Remarks and references to Appendices
LE SOUICH	1		During the forenoon the Battalion was engaged in a scheme of attack on LE SOUICH from IVERGNY. Officers and N.C.Os of the Battalion attended a lecture at POMMERA by Capt. WEIR of the 2nd TANK Brigade on "Co-operation between Infantry and Tanks."	
	2		Battalion training and on range practices.	
	3/6		In the training area this period was mainly taken up with Battalion and Brigade tactical exercises in which an enemy was represented. A Contact Aeroplane, Guns and the Divisional Artillery and a Company of the 33rd Battalion Machine Gun Corps took part on the 6th. Officers and Platoon Sergeants attended a Tank Demonstration at WAVRANS on 5th Septr.	
	7		Training and recreation.	
	8		Church service parades only.	
	9/13		This period was devoted to training, including co-operation with tanks (imaginary), lectures etc. On 13th Septr. the G.O.C. 33rd Division addressed all Officers, Warrant Officers and N.C.Os of the Brigade outside LE SOUICH.	
	14		On this date the Battalion embussed with the Brigade Group at 9 p.m. on LE SOUICH - IVERGNY ROAD and proceeded to ETRICOURT, where guides were met from 21st Division. Group Transport under C.O. No 3 Coy. Train moved by stages during 14th to 16th September by road via DOULLENS and ALBERT to LE TRANSLOY, thence forward area.	
	15		Surplus /	

Army Form C. 2118.

WAR DIARY
or
INTELLIGENCE SUMMARY.
(Erase heading not required.)

Summary of Events and Information SEPTEMBER, 1918.

Place	Date	Hour		Remarks and references to Appendices
5TH SCOTTISH RIFLES.	15		Surplus and Minimum Reserve personnel encamped at BEAULENCOURT and remainder of Battalion (less Transport) at EQUANCOURT. Orders were received for the Battalion at maximum strength of 25 Other Ranks per Platoon, inclusive of Platoon Headquarters but exclusive of Company Headquarters - to relieve the 1st Wiltshire Regiment on the night of 14th/15th September in the HEUDECOURT Sector. Relief completed as follows by 3.20 a.m. 16th September:- Right Front "D" Company. Centre "A" " Left Front "C" " Support "B" "	
	16		On the night of 16th/17th September the Battalion was relieved as follows:- "D" Company by 2 Companies 9th Duke of Wellington's Regiment front being extended to the right. "A" Company by one company 12th Manchester Regiment. "C" Coy & 2 Platoons of B Coy by 2 Coys 1st Manchester Regt. "B" Company in Support by 1 Company 12th Manchester Regiment and 1 Company 9th Duke of Wellington's Regiment (52nd and 62nd Infantry Brigades.) Relief was completed by 4 a.m. 17th September and Companies thereafter marched to ETRICOURT and bivouacked there.	
	17		Lt. A.B.McCRAE, M.C., was killed by a shell on the road. Battalion Transport Lines established at EQUANCOURT. Troops allowed to rest and afterwards clean up.	
	18		At 6 a.m. Battalion moved to position of assembly in the Trench system and sunken roads - left of EQUANCOURT defences - and remained there throughout the day.	
	19		At 7 a.m. the Battalion moved to low ground about W 19 d (Sh.57 c S.E.) 1,000 yards N.E. of PEIZIERS, in artillery formation. At 10 p.m. guides were met and conducted Companies forward to the Support positions in Brown and	

Army Form C. 2118.

WAR DIARY
or
INTELLIGENCE SUMMARY.
(Erase heading not required.)

5TH SCOTTISH RIFLES. Summary of Events and Information **SEPTEMBER, 1918.**

Place	Date	Hour	Summary of Events and Information	Remarks and references to Appendices
	19		and Green Lines near VAUCELETTE Farm) where they relieved units of the 2nd Lincolns Regiment and 12th/13th Northumberland Fusiliers (62nd Infantry Brigade)	
	20		The Battalion was occupied in improving their positions and trenches and approaches in front were reconnoitred.	
	21		At 5.40 a.m. an attack in conjunction with neighbouring units was started by the 19th Infantry Brigade on the right and the 98th Infantry Brigade on the left of the Divisional Front. The 5th Scottish Rifles were in Brigade Reserve and at ZERO minus 30 mins. moved two Companies to PLANE TRENCH and thence to sunken road in X 20 b and d. The attacking Battalions of the Brigade failed to secure their objectives. Carrying parties from "A" Company were supplied. In the afternoon orders were received by the Battalion to be prepared to attack on the same front. At 7.18 p.m. C and D Companies went forward to the assault of MEATH POST and trenches to N and S of it, after capture of which they were to push forward to GLOSTER ROAD. At 7.45 p.m. the Companies were close up to the barrage and MEATH POST was captured. Many casualties were inflicted on the enemy and 3 officers 1 Sergeant Major and 38 men taken prisoner. Patrols were established on East side of GLOSTER ROAD and defensive flanks formed as they were not in touch with our own troops. The objectives were taken with great dash and comparatively light casualties. In the operations Lieut. J.P.MILLAR was killed and Captain N.M. ROBERTSON-SMITH and 2/Lieut. C.S.McDONALD wounded. Lieuts. N. CLARK and J.H.MACPHERSON though slightly wounded remained at duty.	
	22		Advanced posts had to be withdrawn from GLOSTER ROAD owing to enemy fire from the flanks. Companies consolidated and held their new positions.	
	23		On the night of 22nd/23rd the Battalion was relieved by 16th K.R.R.C. Relief/	

Army Form C. 2118.

WAR DIARY
or
INTELLIGENCE SUMMARY.
(Erase heading not required.)

Instructions regarding War Diaries and Intelligence Summaries are contained in F. S. Regs., Part II. and the Staff Manual respectively. Title pages will be prepared in manuscript.

5TH SCOTTISH RIFLES.   Summary of Events and Information   **SEPTEMBER, 1918.**

Place	Date	Hour	Summary of Events and Information	Remarks and references to Appendices
	23		Relief was completed by 3.20 a.m. and Companies marched direct to bivouacs 1,000 yards S.W. of FINS where Battalion rested for the day.	
	24		The Battalion cleaned up and was inspected on parade by the Division General (Sir Reginald PINNEY, K.C.B.) who complimented all ranks on the successful battle they had fought.	
	25		The day was given over to interior economy and making up of deficiencies as far as possible.	
	26		Orders received for relief of 1st Middlesex by the Battalion on the night of the 26/27th. At 10 a.m. it moved to open ground S.W. of HEUDECOURT and remained there till 7.30 p.m. when Companies set out at intervals and were led by guides to MEUNIER Trench and Support on Southern edge of VILLERS GUISLAIN. Relief was carried out quietly and without incident.	
	27		Quiet day in the line. Ground reconnoitred and orders issued with a view to participating on the right flank of an attack by 98th Brigade (2/A. & S.H. on the right) with objectives N and E of VILLERS GUISLAIN.	
	28		Sniping and Artillery activity on both sides. C.O. 1st Middlesex informed of plans for attack on the Battalion front and preparations made for handing over to 1st Middlesex Regiment. Relief completed by 10 p.m. Companies occupied RACKET TRENCH and communications with Battalion Headquarters in VAUCELETTE Farm.	
	29		Battalion held in ready support to 98th Brigade but no action called for.	
	30		During the early morning the enemy withdrew from the area W of the Canal /	

Army Form C. 2118.

WAR DIARY
or
INTELLIGENCE SUMMARY.
(Erase heading not required.)

5TH SCOTTISH RIFLES. Summary of Events and Information SEPTEMBER, 1918.

Place	Date	Hour	Summary of Events and Information	Remarks and references to Appendices
	30		CANAL and took up his main position E of HONNECOURT. Battalion on 30 minutes notice – Dispositions unaltered.	
			CASUALTIES DURING MONTH.	
			Officers. Other Ranks.	
			Lieut. A.B.McCRAE, M.C. killed in action 17/9/18. Killed in action 13.	
			Lieut. J.P.MILLAR, killed in action 21/9/18. Wounded. 127.	
			Capt. N.M.ROBERTSON-SMITH, wounded 21/9/18. Wounded & Missing. 3.	
			2/Lieut. C.S.MACDONALD, wounded 21/9/18. Missing. 15.	
			Lt. N. CLARK, M.M. wounded at duty 22/9/18. Wounded at duty. 10.	
			Lt. R. DICK, wounded at duty 22/9/18.	
			Lt. J.H.MACPHERSON do. do.	
			REINFORCEMENT RECEIVED.	
			Lieut. J.P.MILLER joined for duty 14/9/18. 37	
			STRENGTH OF BATTALION.	
			Officers 40. Other Ranks 698.	
			[signature]	
			Lieut.-Col. Commanding 5th Scottish Rifles.